The Bible Story Hour

BY LOUISA M. JOHNSTON

ILLUSTRATED BY ANNA MARIE MAGAGNA

MANA R: ANNE NEIGOFF

STANDARD EDUCATIONAL CORPORATION

Chicago 1985

Library of Congress Cataloging in Publication Data
Johnston, Louisa Mae.
  The Bible story hour.
  SUMMARY: A retelling of forty-six Bible stories
from the Old and New Testaments.
  1. Bible stories, English. [1. Bible stories]
I. Magagna, Anna Marie, illus. II. Title.
BS551.2.J6   220.9'505   74-9831
ISBN 0-87392-002-3

To the Reader

IT WAS LONG, LONG AGO that boys and girls first sat and listened to stories from the Bible. In that long-ago time there were no books with beautiful pictures in them. But children then loved to listen to these stories and children today still find that these stories make the most wonderful storybook in the world.

Once there was a shepherd boy who became king. His name was David, and you will find his story here. Once there was a boy called Daniel and he was put in a lion's den. His story is here, too. Once there was a Child who was born in a manger. A great star was shining in the sky and three Wise Men journeyed from far places to bring Him gifts and adore Him. And when that Child grew up, He brought wonderful tidings of great joy to all the world. His story is always new and fresh and we want to hear it again and again.

That is why we bring you this book of Bible stories from the Old and New Testaments, retold just for you. When you are very young, you will like to listen to these stories as your father or mother reads them to you and you look at the colorful, beautiful pictures. When you are older, you will like to curl up in a chair and read them to yourself. For these are growing-up stories, stories to read and reread until their shining message is part of all you think and do and are.

We hope you will love these Bible stories as we do and as boys and girls have loved them through the ages. We hope you will find the Prayers and Graces at the end of the book are Prayers and Graces you want to say, too, to thank God for the wonderful world He has given us.

This is *your* book of Bible stories, retold just for you. We hope they will bring you many happy hours.

Contents

Contents

GENESIS 1:1 *In the beginning God created the heaven and the earth.*

The Beginning of God's Wonderful World

A LONG, LONG TIME AGO, longer than you or I can imagine, there was no wonderful world. There were none of the many things we see about us every day.

When you close your eyes and see nothing at all you can guess what it was like to have no beautiful green grass, no bright sun, no gay birds or flowers, and no people.

But even as long ago as this there was God. And God made the world we live in. He gave it all the beautiful things we see about us every day. God made the heavens above us and the earth we walk on.

At first the earth was dark. Then God made light for the day. The darkness was the night.

Then God made the land and the water. And where there was land, God made the grass grow upon it and the trees and the flowers and all the things that grow.

God made the sun and the moon and the stars. He made fish and birds and animals of all kinds. Last of all He made man and woman and He gave all the wonderful things of the earth to them.

8

When we look around us at all
the beautiful things that God has
made we know that we have much
for which we should thank Him.
We know our whole wonderful
world is a gift from God.

GENESIS 3:23 *Therefore the Lord God sent him forth from the garden of Eden, to till the ground from whence he was taken.*

Adam and Eve

GOD GAVE A WONDERFUL WORLD to the first man and woman. He put them in a beautiful garden called Eden. There were many good fruits to eat and there was pure water to drink. The man and the woman had everything they needed to make them happy.

There was only one thing the man and woman must not do.

In the center of the garden there was a tree. This tree was different from any other tree in the garden.

"You may eat of all the other trees," God had said. "But of this tree, you must not eat."

There were many other trees in the garden. The man and woman ate of their fruit and were happy. But as time went by there came a serpent to the garden. He talked to the woman.

"Can you eat of every tree in the garden?" he asked.

10

"We may eat of all the trees but one," she said and pointed to the tree in the center of the garden. "If we touch that tree or eat of it, we will die. God has told us so."

The serpent said, "You shall not die. For God knows that the day you eat of its fruit, your eyes will be opened and you will be as gods, knowing good and evil."

So when the woman saw that the tree was good for food and that it was pleasant to the eyes and could make one wise, she took of its fruit and ate. Then she gave some of its fruit to her husband and he ate.

After they ate their eyes were opened and they were ashamed. They took big leaves and covered themselves.

Then they heard the voice of God in the garden. For the first time, they were frightened of Him and hid.

God called Adam. "Where are you?"

The man said, "I heard your voice in the garden, and I was afraid."

God said, "Why were you afraid? Have you eaten of the tree that I commanded you should not eat?"

The man said, "The woman Thou gave to be with me gave me fruit of the tree and I ate."

Then God said to the woman, "What have you done?"

The woman said, "The serpent tempted me and I ate."

Then God said to the serpent, "Because you did this, you shall crawl in the dust all the days of your life."

God told the man and woman they would be punished for what they had done. They would know pain and would have to work hard to live. Because they had disobeyed God, they would have to leave the garden forever.

God made clothes of skins for Adam and Eve. Then they were sent away from the beautiful garden forever.

GENESIS 13:15 *For all the land which thou seest, to thee will I give it, and to thy seed for ever.*

Abraham's Long Journey

AS THE YEARS went by more and more people lived upon the earth. They built great cities and traveled to far places. As they did this, they came to think more and more about themselves and less and less of God. In time they began to think there were many gods. They made images of the gods and prayed to them.

This was the way the people of Ur in the land of Chaldea lived. Their beautiful city was filled with large buildings, but the largest and most beautiful of all was the temple of the moon god. The people prayed to the moon god when they were happy and when they were sad or afraid. Often they prayed that the great river that ran by the city would not overflow again and bring death to the people of Ur.

14

Not all the people of Ur wanted to live this way. Terah, the great chief of his people, was sad at heart when he saw how the people bowed down to idols. Although he was an old man, he decided to take his family away to a new land.

"We will go to the land of Canaan," he said.

Terah and his son Abraham and Abraham's wife, Sarah, and his grandson Lot began to make ready for the journey.

There was much to do for Terah and his family had many tents and flocks of sheep. They began to roll up the tents and gather all the sheep together. At last the time came to begin the long journey to Canaan. Sheep and camels and donkeys, men and women and children started along the banks of the river toward the city of Haran.

At Haran the people and their flocks rested. They were
weary of traveling and they did not want to start another
long trip. They settled in Haran and while they stayed there
Terah died. He did not live to see Canaan.

Then Terah's son Abraham put on the robe of the chief.

One night in a dream God spoke to Abraham.

God told Abraham to leave Haran and God would bring him
to a land where his children would become a great nation.

The next day Abraham called the people together and told
them that they would travel on.

Again the people made ready for a long journey. They took down their tents and rolled them up. They gathered the flocks of sheep together. When all was ready, Abraham and his people set out along the edge of the desert.

After many months of hard travel the people came to the land of Canaan. Here they found good grazing land and water for the sheep. At last they had a new home where they could worship God as they pleased.

God told Abraham that this was the land he and his people had been given. Abraham looked over the country. He saw the green grass and the clear water and he was happy.

He built an altar to God and thanked Him for bringing the people of Abraham to the new land.

GENESIS 22:17 *I will multiply thy seed as the stars of the heaven, and as the sand which is upon the sea shore.*

Rebekah Comes to the Well

ABRAHAM HAD MUCH to make him a happy man. God had given him a good land to live in. He had many servants and sheep and a wife he loved. But there was one thing that Abraham wanted that he did not have.

Abraham had no son.

Yet God had promised Abraham that his children would become a great nation.

One night when Abraham looked up at the stars God spoke to him. Again He told Abraham that his children's children would be as many as the stars in the sky. This was so many that no man could count them.

18

But how could this be? Abraham was an old man and still he had no son.

At last God told Abraham wonderful news. And one day there was great joy in Abraham's home. A baby boy was born! Abraham named his son Isaac, which means laughter. That was his way of showing his happiness at God's great goodness to him and his wife.

As the boy Isaac grew older, Abraham taught him about God and told him of God's promises. Abraham and Sarah and Isaac loved each other and were happy. Then after many years, Sarah died.

Now Abraham and Isaac were lonely. Abraham was a very old man. He knew that soon he, too, might die. Then Isaac would have no family of his own. How sad he would be!

Abraham loved his son and wanted him to be happy. How could he help him?

"Isaac is a young man now," he thought. "If he had a wife, he would have someone of his own. Then he would not be so lonely."

Abraham called his most trusted servant to him.

"Go back to my old home," he said. "Find a wife for my son Isaac and bring her back here."

The servant promised that he would do as Abraham asked. He took ten of Abraham's camels and many beautiful gifts and went back to where Abraham had lived. It was evening when he came there and he made the camels kneel down beside a well outside the city.

Soon a beautiful girl came to draw water from the well.

The servant said to her, "Please give me a little water."

At once the girl gave him water to drink. Then the man knew that she was kind and gentle as well as beautiful. He was sure that God had led him to her.

The girl's name was Rebekah. The servant went to her home with her. He told her and her father his story and Rebekah said she would go with him and be Isaac's wife.

Meanwhile Isaac waited and waited. One evening he went out into the fields to think. He looked up and he saw camels coming toward him.

Rebekah was on one of the camels. How long the journey must have seemed to her!

"Who is that man coming to meet us?" she asked.

The servant told her that it was Isaac.

Rebekah's journey was over. Now Isaac had a wife. He loved Rebekah. He was no longer lonely.

Abraham was happy for his son. He told Isaac again of God's promises. He told him to listen for God's voice and to be a good chief to his people.

Soon after this Abraham died. Isaac became the leader of his people.

Isaac was a good chief. He took good care of his people and remembered the rights of all. Isaac remembered the way his father had taught him and worshiped God and did his best to do God's bidding.

GENESIS 27:38 *And Esau said unto his father, Hast thou but one blessing, my father? Bless me, even me also, O my father.*

Is This Jacob or Esau?

ABRAHAM AND SARAH had waited a long time for a son. Isaac and Rebekah also waited a long time for children. You can imagine then how happy they were when twin sons were born!

The boys were named Esau and Jacob. Although the boys were twins, they were different in the way they looked and in the things they liked to do.

Esau was strong and hairy and he liked to go hunting. He grew up to be a mighty hunter.

Jacob was a quiet boy with smooth skin. He liked to tend the sheep and to spend the time close to his father's tents.

Esau was his father's favorite, but his mother loved Jacob best.

Esau and Jacob were so very different that they did not get along well together.

Besides, even though they were twins, Esau was just a little older than Jacob. He was the first-born son of Isaac and in that time this meant that Esau would get most of his father's riches when Isaac died.

Jacob knew this, and he did not feel it was right. Why should his twin brother have more than he would have?

One day Esau took his bow and arrows and went hunting. When he came back, he was very tired and hungry.

Jacob had just made a soup. How good it smelled to hungry Esau!

"Let me have some of your fine soup," Esau said to Jacob. "I am so hungry!"

Jacob smiled.

"You may have all the soup," Jacob said, "but first you must give me your birthright."

Esau was so very hungry he promised Jacob that he could have the birthright. To Esau the food he wanted right now was more important than riches in the future.

Isaac was old. He knew that one day he would die. Before he died, he wanted to be sure Esau had his special blessing— the special blessing that a father gave to his first-born son.

He called Esau to him.

"Take your bow and arrow and bring me some meat," he said. "Cook the meat the way you know I like it best. Then I will give you my blessing."

Rebekah heard Isaac tell Esau this. As soon as Esau went hunting for the meat, Rebekah went to Jacob.

"Go quickly and bring meat," she told him. "I will fix the meat the way your father likes it best. Then you will take it to him, and he will give you his special blessing."

Jacob wanted his father's blessing. Esau had promised Jacob his birthright, but Jacob wanted the blessing, too. But would Isaac give it to him?

"My father is old and blind," Jacob said, "but even so he will know that I am not Esau if I bring him meat. I do not dress as Esau does, and Esau is a hairy man and I am not."

"Bring the meat," Rebekah said. "We will dress you in Esau's clothes and put the skins of animals over your hands and neck. Then your father will think you are Esau."

Jacob listened to his mother. Then he went and took two young sheep from the flock and brought them to Rebekah. Rebekah cooked the meat the way Isaac liked it best.

Then Jacob dressed in Esau's clothes and put the skins of animals over his hands and neck, and took the meat to his father.

"I am Esau, your first-born son," Jacob told his father. "I have done as you told me. Now sit up and eat of my game that you may bless me."

Isaac was old and blind.

"Come near," he said, "that I may feel you, my son, so I can know if you are Esau or not."

Jacob came near and Isaac felt him but the clothes and animal skins Jacob wore fooled him.

"The voice is the voice of Jacob," Isaac said, "but the hands are the hands of Esau."

Then he gave Jacob his special blessing because he thought he was Esau.

Soon afterward Esau came with the meat he had prepared. But it was too late. Jacob had tricked Isaac into giving him the special blessing.

How angry Esau was! In his anger, he hated his brother and wanted to kill him.

GENESIS 33:4 *And Esau ran to meet him, and embraced him, and fell on his neck, and kissed him: and they wept.*

Jacob's Dream

REBEKAH KNEW that Esau was very angry. She knew that Jacob must go away to be safe.

She went to Isaac. "It is time Jacob had a wife," she said. "Let us send him to my brother Laban in Haran. He can find a wife there."

Soon Jacob was on his way to Haran. It was a long journey, and Jacob was lonely. He began to think of what he had done to his brother Esau, and he was sorry and ashamed.

One night while Jacob rested in a field, he had a wonderful dream. In the dream, he saw a ladder that climbed from earth to heaven. Angels were going up and down the ladder. At the top of the ladder was God.

God told Jacob that the land where he slept would belong to him some day. God told him He would be with him wherever he went and that He would bring Jacob to this land again.

When Jacob woke from his wonderful dream, he took the stone he had used for a pillow and set it upright. He poured oil on its top and promised God he would serve Him.

Jacob traveled on to Haran, but he was no longer lonely. He knew God was with him.

At last Jacob came to the home of his uncle Laban. There he saw Rachel, Laban's daughter, and loved her and wanted to marry her.

"If you will work for me seven years," Laban said, "I will let you marry Rachel."

Jacob loved Rachel, so he agreed. He worked hard for Laban, but just as Jacob had cheated his brother, so Laban cheated Jacob. When the seven years were over, Laban married Jacob to his older daughter, Leah. He told Jacob that if he wanted to marry Rachel, he must work seven more years.

Jacob loved Rachel so much that he agreed to work for Laban seven more years. He and Rachel were married. Jacob had children and many sheep and goats. Only one thing made him unhappy. He wanted to return home and ask his brother Esau to forgive him.

At last Jacob decided he must go home. He must go and
see his brother again and ask him to forgive him.

Jacob called his family together and told them to get ready
for the long journey back to Canaan. When all was ready,
Jacob put his wives and children on camels, and they started
on their way, driving the cattle before them. There were men
and women and children, sheep and goats and donkeys. What
a long caravan they made!

When they came close to Jacob's old home, he sent men
ahead to tell Esau that Jacob was coming. Jacob sent many
gifts with these messengers, for he wanted Esau to know that
he was coming in peace and friendship.

But when the messengers came back, they told Jacob that
Esau was coming to meet him with four hundred men.

Then Jacob was filled with fear. Was his brother still angry with him? Did Esau still hate him and want to kill him? Would he try to harm Jacob and his family?

But Jacob did not turn back. He still wanted to go home. He wanted his brother Esau's forgiveness.

But he loved his family, too. How could he protect them if Esau was still angry? Jacob thought and thought. Then he divided all the people into two groups. He divided the flocks and herds and camels, too, and put part with one group and part with the other group.

Now if Esau were angry and tried to hurt one group, the other could still escape.

Jacob prayed to God and asked for His help and protection.

Then he watched his brother and his brother's men come nearer and nearer.

Then, all alone, Jacob went to meet his brother Esau. As he came closer, he bowed down seven times and asked Esau to forgive him.

But Esau ran to meet his brother and put his arms around his neck and welcomed him back.

How surprised Esau was when he saw Jacob's family and all his flocks and herds! He was surprised, too, at the rich gifts Jacob wanted to give him.

But Esau did not want to take the gifts.

Esau said, "I have enough, my brother. Keep what you have for yourself."

But Jacob begged Esau to take the gifts as a sign that his brother had forgiven him. Then Esau took them.

Esau wanted Jacob to travel on with him toward home. But Jacob had many children and women and flocks with him.

"You go on," he told his brother. "We will follow after you for we must go more slowly than you and your men can travel."

Esau went on. Soon Jacob would follow him home. It was enough for Jacob now that he and his brother had made their peace and were friends at last.

GENESIS 37:5 *Joseph dreamed a dream, and he told it to his brethren: and they hated him yet the more.*

Joseph and His Brothers

JACOB TRAVELED ON to the land of Canaan and there he and his family set their tents and made their home. Many years passed and Jacob's sons were young men. Jacob loved all his sons, but there was one son he loved the best. His name was Joseph.

When Joseph was seventeen years old, his father made him a coat of many colors.

Now the other brothers knew that their father loved Joseph best. It made them jealous and unhappy. When they saw the beautiful coat of many colors, they were even more unhappy. They were angry with Joseph and hated him.

Then Joseph had a dream and told it to his brothers.

"In my dream," he said, "we were binding sheaves in the field and my sheaf rose and stood upright. Then all your sheaves gathered around it and bowed down to it."

31

His brothers were angry. "What does this mean?" they asked. "Do you think you will rule over all of us?"

Joseph dreamed again and again he told his dream to his brothers.

"I dreamed that the sun, the moon, and eleven stars bowed down to me," he said.

Now even Jacob, Joseph's father, was troubled.

"What is this dream?" he asked. "Shall we all—I and your mother and your brothers —come to bow down to you?"

The dream troubled Jacob and he thought of it often. But the dream made Joseph's brothers even more angry.

One day while the brothers were away in the pastures with the flocks of sheep, Jacob called Joseph to him.

"Go," he said, "and see if it is well with your brothers and the flocks. Then bring word to me how they are."

Joseph went to look for his brothers. While he was still a long way off, they saw him coming in his coat of many colors. They remembered his dreams and were full of anger.

"Here comes the dreamer," they said. "Let us take and kill him and throw him in a pit. Then we shall see what happens to his dreams!"

Reuben, the eldest brother, did not want to hurt Joseph.

"Do not kill him," he said. "Let us just throw him into a pit and leave him here in the wilderness."

For Reuben thought that later he could come and take Joseph from the pit and bring him safely home.

His brothers did not know of his secret plan. They liked what he had said.

"We will not kill Joseph," they agreed. "We will put him in a pit and leave him there."

When Joseph came near, the brothers tore off his coat of many colors. They threw him in a pit.

Then Reuben left to look after some of the flock.

While he was gone, the brothers sat down to eat. A caravan came along with many camels loaded with gum and myrrh and balm to sell in Egypt.

When they saw the caravan, the brothers had an idea.

"Let us sell Joseph to the traders for a slave!" they said.

Reuben was not there to stop them. Quickly the brothers drew Joseph out of the pit. They sold him to the traders.

When Reuben returned and found Joseph gone, he was filled with fear and grief.

"What shall we do?" he cried. "How shall I tell my father?"

But his brothers had thought of this, too. They took Joseph's coat of many colors and dipped it in the blood of an animal they had killed.

Then they brought the coat to Jacob, their father.

When Jacob saw the coat, he wept.

"It is my son's coat," he said. "A wild animal has killed him!" And he would not be comforted.

But Joseph was not dead. The traders had taken him to Egypt. There they sold him to Potiphar, the captain of the Pharaoh's guard.

GENESIS 41:41　*And Pharaoh
said unto Joseph, See, I have set
thee over all the land of Egypt.*

Joseph and
the Great Pharaoh

JOSEPH WAS IN A STRANGE LAND far from his own home and
people. Can you imagine how lonely and afraid he must have
been?

But Potiphar, the captain of the Pharaoh's guard, was good
to Joseph. Even though Joseph was his slave, Potiphar came to
trust him and believe in him.

He found that Joseph could help him in many ways. Soon
he made Joseph overseer of his house and all he owned.

Now there was trouble at the palace of the Pharaoh, the ruler of all Egypt. Pharaoh had had a bad dream and although he asked all his wise men to tell him what the dream meant, they could not do so.

One day Pharaoh heard of Joseph. He heard that Joseph had told many people the meaning of dreams and that always what Joseph said came true.

"Send Joseph to me," Pharaoh ordered.

When the message from the great Pharaoh came, Joseph put on his finest clothes and went to the palace. Soon he was brought before Pharaoh.

Pharaoh said, "I have dreamed a dream and no one can tell me what it means. Can you tell me its meaning?"

Joseph said, "It is not in me to give you an answer. God shall give Pharaoh an answer."

36

Pharaoh said, "In my dream seven fat cows came out of the river and fed in the grass. Then seven thin cows came and ate the fat cows. But the seven thin cows were still as thin as before."

Then Joseph said, "God is telling Pharaoh what is going to happen. The seven fat cows are seven years of good harvests when there will be plenty and more than plenty for the people to eat. And the seven thin cows are seven years of bad harvests when nothing will grow and people will be hungry."

"What shall I do?" Pharaoh asked.

Joseph said, "God is telling you what will happen soon. Now you can find a man who is good and wise. He can take part of the good harvest for each of the seven good years and put it away. Then when the seven years of bad harvests come, there will still be food for the people to eat."

Pharaoh said to Joseph, "Since God has shown you all of this, there is no one as wise as you. You shall be over my house and my people. You shall tell all Egypt what to do and they shall do it. Only I will be greater than you."

So Joseph went out over all the land of Egypt and told the people what to do and the people did it. Just as the dream had foretold, seven years of good harvests came when there was plenty and more than plenty for the people to eat.

And each year, Joseph took part of the good harvest and stored it away safely.

Then the good years were over. The bad years came when the harvests were poor and little would grow.

Pharaoh's dream had come true. All that Joseph had said would happen had happened.

In all the lands around Egypt, people were hungry. But in Egypt, the people had food to eat because Joseph had stored it safely away for them.

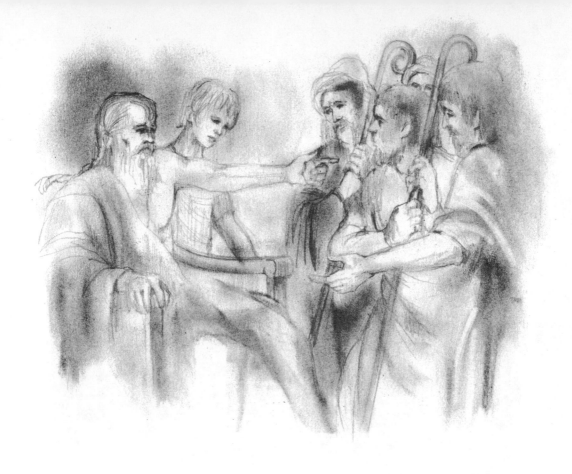

GENESIS 45:28 *And Israel said, It is enough; Joseph my son is yet alive: I will go and see him before I die.*

A Joyful Meeting in Egypt

IN THE YEARS THAT FOLLOWED there was bread to eat in Egypt, but in the countries around Egypt there was little to eat. The people were hungry. Many came to Egypt to buy grain.

In the land where Joseph's people lived there was hunger, too. Jacob, Joseph's father, called his sons to him.

"I hear there is grain in the land of Egypt," he said. "Go down to Egypt and buy grain that we may live and not die."

So ten of Joseph's brothers went to Egypt to buy grain. But Jacob did not send Benjamin, his youngest son, for he was only a boy. Jacob loved him very much and feared for him on the journey.

In Egypt, the brothers went to Joseph who was governor of the land. They bowed down and asked to buy grain.

When Joseph saw his brothers bow down before him, he remembered his dream of long ago. He saw, too, that they did not know him. He pretended he did not know them and spoke roughly to them.

"You are spies," he said. "I will not believe you are honest men unless you prove it to me."

Then he set a hard test for them, for he wanted to find out if they were truly sorry for what they had done to him when they sold him into slavery.

"You may go home," he told them, "and take grain with you to feed your hungry people. But you must leave one brother here in prison. Then you must come back and bring your youngest brother with you."

The brothers did not want to do this but what else could they do? Sadly they went home to Canaan.

They told their father Jacob all that had happened and what Joseph demanded of them.

Jacob was filled with sorrow and fear. He had lost one son and one was a prisoner in Egypt. Must he lose his youngest son, Benjamin, too?

But when the grain the brothers had brought back to Canaan was gone and the people were hungry again, Jacob knew what he must do. The brothers must go back to Egypt for grain and he must send Benjamin with them.

With a sad heart, Jacob said goodbye to his sons.

Taking Benjamin with them, the brothers went back to Egypt.

How glad Joseph was when he saw his young brother! But still he did not let his brothers know who he was, for he was not sure yet that they were truly sorry for the wrong they had done him.

He let his other brother out of prison. But he set other hard tests for his brothers. Each time they proved that they were honest men.

Then Joseph knew that they were good men now and sorry for the wrong they had done. He could not hide the truth from them any longer.

He asked all the other people around him to leave and he told his brothers who he was.

"I am your brother, Joseph," he said, "whom you sold into Egypt. And now you must not be sorry or angry with yourselves for doing that. For God sent me here before you so that there might be food for the people to eat."

How surprised Joseph's brothers were! At first they could hardly believe it was he and that he was not angry with them.

Joseph asked, "Is my father truly alive?"

Then the brothers rejoiced together and told each other all that had happened in the long years since they were parted.

When Pharaoh heard that Joseph's brothers had come, he rejoiced, too.

Pharaoh told Joseph, "Tell your brothers to load their animals and go home. And when they come to the land of Canaan, they must take your father and all the family and their belongings and bring them to Egypt."

And Pharaoh promised to give them land and riches in the land of Egypt.

So Joseph's brothers went back to the land of Canaan. They told Jacob the happy news.

"Joseph is still alive," they told him, "and he is governor over all the land of Egypt."

At first Jacob could hardly believe them. But when they told him all that Joseph had said and he saw the fine things Joseph had sent him, Jacob knew that they spoke the truth.

"It is enough," he said. "Joseph my son is still alive. I will go and see him before I die."

So all of Joseph's family came to live in Egypt. They spent many happy years together there. But sometimes they thought of their own land and wanted to return.

EXODUS 2:10 *And the child grew, and she brought him unto Pharaoh's daughter, and he became her son. And she called his name Moses: and she said, Because I drew him out of the water.*

The Baby Moses

JOSEPH DIED, but his people lived on in Egypt. His people, the people of Israel, tended their sheep on the hillsides and were strong and happy. Their children laughed under the sun.

Many, many years passed and a new Pharaoh became ruler of Egypt. He did not know Joseph. He did not remember how Joseph had saved the people of Egypt from hunger.

The new Pharaoh saw only that there were now a great many of Joseph's people in his land. He saw that they were strong, and he was afraid.

"Look!" said Pharaoh. "See how many people of Israel there are among us! See how strong they are. What if there were a war and they fought against us? We must make sure that they do not grow stronger."

He gave a new order. He commanded that the people of Israel must work for Pharaoh.

Now Joseph's people were no longer free to tend their sheep on the hillside or work for themselves. Pharaoh set men over them to make them work from early morning till late at night. Under the hot sun, the people of Israel worked with bricks and mortar to build a city for Pharaoh.

"Work faster!" Pharaoh's men shouted to the people of Israel. "Work harder! You cannot stop to rest."

But still Joseph's people were sturdy and strong. Still their families grew and grew.

Pharaoh was angry. How could he keep these people from growing stronger?

He gave another order to the people of Joseph.

"From now on," he told them, "every son that is born to you, you must throw into the river. But every daughter you shall let live."

Imagine how unhappy all the people of Israel were when they heard Pharaoh's command! How could they put their own baby boys into the river to die?

The people of Israel were afraid of Pharaoh. But they loved their baby sons. They would not kill them.

Pharaoh was very angry. He told his soldiers to look for the babies and kill them.

How afraid the fathers and mothers of Israel were now! How could they save their babies?

One mother hid her baby boy. When he was very little, she hid him in the house. But as the baby grew older and stronger, his cries grew stronger and louder. What if the people in the street heard him? Then they would find him and he would be killed.

The mother made a brave plan. She took bulrushes from the river and made a strong basket. Then she spread a thick covering of pitch over it. Now no water could get into the basket.

When the basket was finished, the mother made a soft place inside it for the baby and wrapped him warmly in his finest blanket. She held him tightly for a minute and whispered a prayer to God. Then she put him in the basket.

"Come," she said to his sister Miriam, and in the gray light of early morning, they crept out and carried the basket down to the river.

"Watch!" she told Miriam. "Nobody must see us."

While Miriam kept watch, the mother parted the tall plants that grew along the river bank. She slid the basket into the water.

The little basket rocked gently on the quiet waters.

"Hide nearby," the mother said to Miriam. "Watch the basket. If anybody comes near it, come and tell me."

The mother stole away.
Miriam hid among the tall
plants along the river edge.
She watched the basket.

The baby was good. He
did not cry. The little basket
rocked to and fro.

As Miriam watched, she
heard voices and laughter.
Who was coming? Would
they see the basket? What
would they do?

Then Miriam's eyes grew
wide. A group of girls was
at the river's edge. Among
them was the princess, the
daughter of the Pharaoh!

50

The princess and her maidens had come to bathe in the river.

The princess saw the basket.

"Look!" she said. "What is that rocking in the river, close to the shore? Bring it to me."

One of her maidens brought the basket from the river. The princess knelt and saw the baby in it. As she picked him up, he began to cry.

"Hush!" said the princess softly, and she rocked him in her arms. "See how little he is. Some poor Hebrew mother must have hidden him to keep him safe from the soldiers."

Her voice was tender and kind, and the baby stopped crying. He reached up to her and laughed. The princess laughed, too, and held him closer.

"See how strong and beautiful he is!" she said. "See how he laughs and is not afraid. I will keep him, and he will be my son."

Miriam had watched and listened. Now she ran out from her hiding place.

"Princess!" she said eagerly. "Please. I know of a Hebrew woman who will take care of the baby for you. Please let me bring her to nurse the baby."

Pharaoh's daughter smiled at Miriam.

"Go and bring her," she said. "I will give him the name of Moses for I have taken him from the water. He shall be my son."

Miriam did not wait another moment. With flying feet, she ran home to tell her mother. Soon her mother stood before the princess.

The princess put the baby Moses in his own mother's arms.

"Take this baby away and nurse him for me," she said.

How happy the mother of Moses was! Her baby was safe and she could love him and take care of him.

The baby Moses grew into a strong boy. Then it was time for him to go to the princess and be her son. He lived at the court of the Pharaoh and he was taught the things that a prince of Egypt should know.

EXODUS 8:1   *And the Lord spake unto Moses, Go unto Pharaoh, and say unto him, Thus saith the Lord, Let my people go, that they may serve me.*

Let My People Go

MOSES LIVED AS A PRINCE of Egypt, but he did not forget his own people. When he became a man, he tried to help them. Because of this, he was forced to go away. He went to live in a desert place and became a shepherd.

One day while Moses was tending his sheep, he came to a place called Horeb, the mountain of God. There he saw a marvelous sight. A flaming fire came out of a bush, but although the bush burned, it did not burn up.

While Moses looked and wondered, a voice spoke out of the burning bush. It was the voice of God.

God said to Moses, "I am the God of your father, the God of Abraham, the God of Isaac, and the God of Jacob."

Then Moses hid his face, for he was afraid to look at God.

God said to Moses, "I have heard the cry of my people in Egypt. I know their sufferings. I will send you to Pharaoh that you may bring forth the children of Israel out of Egypt."

Moses asked humbly, "Who am I that I should go to Pharaoh, and bring away the people of Israel?"

But God promised to help Moses. He promised to be with Moses and teach him what to do and say. He sent Aaron, the brother of Moses, to help Moses speak to Pharaoh.

And Moses did what God commanded. He and Aaron went before Pharaoh and told him that God wanted him to let the people of Israel leave Egypt.

Pharaoh said, "Who is the Lord that I should listen to Him? I do not know the Lord. I will not let the people of Israel go."

Instead Pharaoh gave orders that the people should work even harder. Now they must not only build with bricks but they must also go and get the straw to make the bricks. And they must accomplish as much as they had done before.

When Moses saw how the people suffered, his heart was full of sadness. He had done what the Lord told him to do, but it had not helped his people. It had only made them suffer more.

Then God told Moses to go again to Pharaoh. God told Moses what to say and do.

Moses went to Pharaoh.

"The Lord, the God of the Hebrews, has sent me," Moses told Pharaoh. "God commanded you to let His people go. You did not obey God. Now God has sent you a sign to show you that He is the Lord. Watch!"

As Pharaoh watched, Moses obeyed God's command. Moses lifted his rod. He struck the waters of the Nile. All the waters turned to blood.

The fish in the river Nile died. The people of Egypt could not drink the water from the Nile. They had to find other water to drink.

54

Seven days passed. Still Pharaoh would not obey God. He would not set the people of Israel free.

Then God sent Moses to Pharaoh again and told him to say, "Thus says the Lord. Let my people go that they may serve me."

But still Pharaoh would not listen. He would not let the people go. Then God sent many plagues to trouble the people of Egypt and show the Pharaoh that he should set the people of Israel free.

First God sent frogs that ran over the land and homes of Egypt. Then he sent lice and swarms of flies into the homes of the people. He made the cattle die and boils form on the Egyptians.

Then hail fell from the sky. The hail fell on the land and spoiled the crops. Clouds of locusts came and ate all the living plants in the fields.

Then darkness came over the land and there was no light.

For three days there was no light over all the land of Egypt.

But still the heart of the Pharaoh was hardened. He would not let the people of Israel go free.

Then the Lord sent a last, terrible plague to the people of Egypt.

The Lord spoke to Moses. "On a certain night I will pass through the land of Egypt. And all the first-born children and animals in the land shall die."

Then God told Moses what the people of Israel must do.

On a certain evening, each family should put the blood of a lamb on the doorpost of the house.

That night the people of Israel must eat the roasted lamb with unleavened bread and bitter herbs.

They must eat quickly and in haste, and they must be dressed for traveling. For in the morning, they would leave Egypt.

The blood of the lamb on the doorpost would be a sign to God.

When God saw the blood of the lamb He would know that these were the houses of His people and He would pass over them.

Moses told the people of Israel all that the Lord had commanded.

"Do as God bids you," he said, "and remember this time forever after with a feast of bitter herbs and unleavened bread and praise to God. For this is the Lord's Passover."

The people of Israel did as God had commanded. And in the night the Lord passed through the land of Egypt and all of the first-born died. Even the first-born child of Pharaoh died.

And there was weeping all through the land.

Pharaoh wept, too. In the middle of that night, he called Moses to him.

Pharaoh said, "Rise up and go from Egypt. Go and serve the Lord. Take your flocks and herds and go!"

And the people of Israel took their belongings and went out from Egypt.

EXODUS 14:22   *And the children of Israel went into the midst of the sea upon the dry ground: and the waters were a wall unto them on their right hand, and on their left.*

The March into the Sea

MOSES AND THE CHILDREN OF ISRAEL left Egypt. But soon after they were gone, Pharaoh began to be sorry that he had let them go.

"What have we done?" he asked. "Who will work for us now as the people of Israel did?"

And he called for his soldiers and his chariots and horses and set out after the people of Israel.

Pharaoh and his army moved swiftly. Soon Pharaoh looked down and saw Moses and his people, camping by the sea.

The people of Israel looked up and saw Pharaoh and his chariots and horses and marching men. And they were in great fear.

They cried out to Moses.

"Do not be afraid," he told them. "The Lord will fight for you. Trust in the Lord and you will be saved."

The Lord did help the people of Israel. He sent a huge pillar of cloud between them and the army of Pharaoh. The cloud and the darkness hid Moses and his people all through the night.

Then at God's command, Moses stretched out his hand over the sea. And the Lord sent a strong east wind to drive back the sea. All night the east wind drove the waters and they divided. In the middle was dry land.

The people of Israel, the men and the women and the children, marched into the sea over the dry land. Walls of water were at their right and at their left.

When day came, God caused the cloud pillar to go away. Pharaoh and his army saw the people of Israel crossing the sea over the path of dry land.

"Follow them!" Pharaoh cried, and his soldiers and his chariots marched into the sea.

Then God commanded Moses to stretch out his hand again. And when Moses put his hand out over the sea, the waters returned. The Egyptians and all their chariots were caught in the rising waters.

The people of Israel were saved! They raised their voices and sang of the glory of God and their faith in Him.

Exodus 19:9   *And the Lord said unto Moses, Lo, I come unto thee in a thick cloud, that the people may hear when I speak with thee, and believe thee for ever.*

The Ten Commandments

MOSES LED THE PEOPLE of Israel away from the Red Sea and into the wilderness. There they wandered for a long time. Often they were tired and thirsty and hungry. Often they were afraid.

But always Moses prayed to the Lord for help and guidance, and always God heard him and helped the people. When they were very thirsty, He sent sweet water to drink. When they were very hungry, He sent food sweet as honey to eat.

After they had wandered for months, the people came into the wilderness of Sinai and camped before a mountain.

There God spoke to Moses and told him of many wonderful things that would come to the people if they would obey God and His commands.

Moses told this to the people.

And they answered, "All that the Lord has spoken, we will do."

Then God told Moses that He would speak to him from a cloud so that all the people could hear. He told Moses to go to the people and help them make themselves ready to hear the Lord.

The people did as God commanded. They made themselves clean in body and heart to hear the words of the Lord.

Two days passed. On the morning of the third day, there was thunder and lightning and a thick cloud covered the mountain. A trumpet blasted loudly and Moses led the people to the foot of the mountain.

As the sound of the trumpet grew louder and louder, Moses spoke and God answered in thunder. He called Moses to come to the top of the mountain.

And there God gave Moses Ten Commandments written on stone tablets to teach the people the good way to live.

These are the Ten Commandments given by God.

I am the Lord thy God which have brought thee out of the land of Egypt, out of the house of bondage. Thou shalt have no other gods before me.

Thou shalt not make unto thee any graven image.

Thou shalt not take the name of the Lord thy God in vain.

Remember the sabbath day, to keep it holy.

Honor thy father and thy mother.

Thou shalt not kill.

Thou shalt not commit adultery.

Thou shalt not steal.

Thou shalt not bear false witness against thy neighbor.

Thou shalt not covet thy neighbor's house, nor any thing that is thy neighbor's.

64

After Moses brought the Ten Commandments down from the mountain, the people of Israel wandered on in the wilderness. They wandered for many years. Sometimes they became sad and discouraged, and they forgot to trust God and obey Him. Then they were sorry and tried again to live as the Lord wanted them to live.

Whenever they went, the people carried the great laws on the stone tablets. They carried the Ten Commandments with them in an Ark they had built according to God's commands.

At last their long journey was almost over. They came close to the river Jordan. Across it lay the Promised Land.

Moses was old now. He knew that he would not cross over the river with his people. He would not set foot in the land God had promised them.

Then the Lord called Moses. He commanded him to go up Mount Nebo. And when Moses went up the mountain, God showed him the beautiful land across the river, the land of Canaan.

Moses saw the Promised Land, and he died, and his people wept as they mourned him.

JOSHUA 6:20   *So the people shouted when the priests blew with the trumpets.*

Joshua and the Walls of Jericho

AFTER THE DEATH OF MOSES, a new leader led the people of Israel. His name was Joshua and he was a bold soldier and mighty warrior.

God commanded Joshua to lead the Hebrew people across the river of Jordan and into the Promised Land, the land of Canaan.

"Be strong and of good courage," the Lord said to Joshua. "Do not be frightened or afraid, for the Lord your God is with you wherever you go."

Joshua did as God commanded.

"Pass through the camp," Joshua told his officers. "Tell the people to prepare food for a journey. We are going to cross over the river of Jordan and into the land God has promised us."

When the people heard Joshua's command, they were filled with surprise and wonder. For this was the harvest time of the year and the waters of the Jordan were deep and ran swiftly, overflowing their banks. How could the people cross the deep river? They had no boats.

But they trusted Joshua. They prepared food to take on the journey. Then they broke camp and moved close to the banks of the river.

For three days, they camped by the river. Then early next morning, they marched to the edge of the swift river.

The priests led the way, carrying the Ark which held the Ten Commandments. Then came the men and the women and children with their donkeys and camels and cattle. After them marched the soldiers of Israel.

The priests walked into the deep waters. As their feet touched them, a wonderful thing happened. The waters from above stopped and formed a high wall. The waters flowing down toward the sea stopped, too. A dry river bed was stretched before the people!

While the priests stood firmly in the river bed, the people of Israel crossed the river of Jordan.

When they were all safely across, God spoke to Joshua.

The Lord said, "Choose twelve men from the people. Tell each man to take a stone from the river, from the place where the priests stood. Carry the twelve stones with you and set them up in the place where you will rest tonight."

Joshua chose twelve men of Israel and the men did as God had commanded. They took the twelve stones from the bed of the river and carried them to the shore.

Then Joshua set up twelve more stones in the river to mark the place where the priests had stood.

When this was done, the priests came out of the river. Then the river waters flowed swiftly again, filling the river bed and overflowing the banks.

The people of Israel set up their tents and camped on the shore of the Jordan. And there, as God had commanded, Joshua set up the twelve stones from the river.

"Remember these stones," he told the people, "and tell your children that they are a sign of how the Lord dried up the waters of the Jordan to let us pass. Tell this again and again so all the peoples of the earth will know the power of the Lord."

The Lord spoke to Joshua again.

As the people camped by the river, they could see the strong walls of the mighty city of Jericho. No one went out of the city and no one went in. The gates of the city were closed against the people of Israel.

But God promised Joshua that the city of Jericho would be taken. He told Joshua what he must do.

Joshua followed God's plan. Once a day for six days, he marched the people around the city. Armed soldiers led the march. Then came seven priests blowing trumpets of rams' horns. The Ark of the Covenant, carried by priests, followed. Then came the people of Israel. Around the city they marched, but the people made no sound. Only the blaring of the trumpets was heard.

For six days this happened. Then it was the seventh day. Very early in the morning, the people marched around the city again. Seven times, they marched around the city and only the trumpets sounded. There was no other sound.

The seventh time the trumpets blared, Joshua called out.

"Shout!" His voice rang out to the people. "The Lord has given you the city!"

A mighty shout rose from the people. And at the great sound, the walls of the city trembled and fell down!

The city of Jericho lay open before the people of Israel. And as God had promised, they went into the city and took it and made it their own.

68

JUDGES 16:28 *And Samson called unto the Lord, and said, O Lord God, remember me, I pray thee, and strengthen me, I pray thee, only this once, O God.*

Samson, the Strong

AFTER THE DAYS OF JOSHUA, the people of Israel had many rulers. As the long years passed, sometimes the people remembered the Lord of their fathers and they followed His commandments. But other times, they forgot God and they worshiped idols. Then God punished them and unhappy times came to them.

Often the people of other nations came to the land of the people of Israel and conquered them. One of these conquering peoples was the nation of the Philistines.

During this time the leaders of the people of Israel were called Judges. One of the most famous of these Judges was Samson.

From the time he was born, Samson lived in a special way to serve God. He did not drink wine. He did not cut his hair, for this was forbidden to him.

70

Samson was a very strong little boy, and as he grew up he became stronger and stronger until no man was as strong as he. One day when Samson went to the vineyards, a roaring lion sprang at him. Samson did not have even a stick or stone to help him, but he was not afraid. He sprang at the fierce lion and killed him with his bare hands.

All the people began to know of Samson and his great strength. The Philistines were afraid of him and tried many times to capture him.

Once the Philistines had Samson bound with strong, new ropes. But the ropes could not hold Samson. He broke free and killed many men.

The Philistines grew more and more afraid of Samson for while he was free, they knew they could not harm his people. For twenty years, Samson ruled his people as a Judge.

But always the Philistines tried to learn the secret of his great strength.

Then Samson made friends with a woman of the Philistines. Her name was Delilah.

The Philistines asked Delilah to find out the secret of Samson's great strength.

Day after day, Delilah asked Samson:

"What is the secret of your great strength?"

Samson laughed and gave her a different reason each time she asked. It was never the true reason.

Then at last one day, Samson grew tired of her many questions. He told her the truth.

"My hair has never been cut," he said. "That is one of the ways I serve the Lord. If my hair is cut, I shall become weak like other men. My great strength will be gone."

Delilah told this to the Philistines.

That night while Samson was sleeping, Delilah had a man come and cut off Samson's long hair. When Samson woke, his great strength was gone, and the Philistines captured him.

They put out his eyes. They put him in prison and set him to grinding grain.

The Philistines were happy then. They had captured the mighty Samson.

One day, the Philistines had a great feast. As they feasted and made merry, they had Samson brought before them.

The Philistines laughed at the blind, stumbling giant.

They saw that while Samson was in prison, his hair had grown long again.

But they did not know that his strength had grown, too. They did not know his mighty strength had returned!

Samson stood between two huge pillars. These pillars held up the house. Samson prayed to the Lord.

"Lord," he prayed. "Let me die with the Philistines."

He took the pillars in his hands and he pulled mightily. With a crash, the house fell on Samson and the Philistines. In this way Samson died and took with him many of the enemies of his people.

RUTH 1:16 *Whither thou go-
est, I will go; and where thou
lodgest, I will lodge: thy people
shall be my people, and thy God
my God.*

The Story of Ruth

IN THE DAYS when the Judges ruled, there came a time when
there was no food and the people of Israel were very hungry.
At that time, there lived a woman called Naomi. Naomi and
her husband and two sons journeyed to the land of Moab for
they had heard there was food there.

Naomi's husband died. Her two sons married girls from
the land of Moab. Then the sons died, too. Naomi was
lonely away from her own people.

"There is food again in my own land," she told her sons'
wives. "I will go back there. But I want you to stay here
with your own people and be happy."

One of the Moab girls kissed Naomi and wept as she
said goodbye. But the other girl clung to Naomi. Her name
was Ruth and she loved Naomi very much.

"Let me go with you," Ruth said to Naomi. "Your home
shall be my home. Your people shall be my people. I will
follow the ways of your God. I want to stay with you always."

Then Naomi kissed Ruth and was glad, for she loved Ruth, too. Together they journeyed to Bethlehem, Naomi's old home. It was harvest time when they reached there and the ears of grain were yellow in the fields.

Ruth saw the men working in the fields, cutting the grain and tying it in bundles. She saw women following the men and picking up the grains they dropped.

"Let me go work in the fields, too," she said to Naomi, for she knew they must have food to eat.

As Ruth worked in the fields, a man stopped to watch her.

The man was called Boaz, and he was the owner of the field where Ruth worked. As he watched Ruth, he wondered about her.

"Who is she?" he asked, and when he heard how she had left her own country to come with Naomi, he wanted to help her.

"Stay in this field," Boaz said to Ruth. "Work here. Here you will be safe."

Shyly Ruth thanked him. How kind he was to a stranger!

At noontime Boaz asked Ruth to eat with him and his men, for he saw that she had no food of her own.

And after Ruth had eaten and gone back to the field to work, Boaz told his men to let her pick up all the grain she could find.

"Pull some grain from your bundles," Boaz told them. "Let her pick up that, too."

When evening came and work was over, Ruth took the grain she had gathered and brought it to Naomi. She told Naomi how kind Boaz had been to her.

"Boaz is our relative," Naomi said. "Work in his field as he told you to do. There you will be safe."

Ruth worked in the fields until harvest was over. Then Naomi made a plan. She wanted Ruth to have a home of her own and be happy. She knew that Boaz liked Ruth.

"There will be a harvest feast," Naomi told Ruth. "When it comes, you must do this."

The night of the harvest feast, Ruth did what Naomi had told her to do. Ruth dressed in her best clothes. After the feast was over, she watched where Boaz lay down to sleep. Then she went quietly and lay at his feet. How surprised Boaz was when he woke and found her there! He spread his robe over her to show he would take care of her.

And Ruth and Boaz were married and lived happily and Naomi was happy, too.

1 SAMUEL 10:24   *And Samuel said to all the people, See ye him whom the Lord hath chosen, that there is none like him among all the people? And all the people shouted, and said, God save the king.*

Saul, the First King of Israel

AFTER THE DEATH of Samson, the people of Israel were ruled for a long time by a wise and just judge called Samuel. As Samuel grew old, there was no one to take his place. Who would rule the people of Israel?

The people looked about them. They saw that other countries had kings. They wanted a king, too.

God told Samuel to warn the people that having a king would not make them happy. But the people would not listen.

So God decided to let the people have their way.

There was a young man among the people called Saul. He was tall and handsome and a brave soldier.

God told Samuel to choose Saul. He would be the first king of Israel.

Samuel called the tribes of Israel together. When all the people were gathered before him, he told Saul to come forward and stand beside him.

"Here is your king," Samuel said. "God has chosen him."

Then all the people shouted, "Long live the king!"

So Saul became the first king of the people of Israel. He was a brave soldier, but he was not a good or wise king. Often he forgot the words of God. He did not always do as God commanded.

At last God decided Saul could no longer be king. There must be a new king of Israel.

"Go to the house of Jesse in Bethlehem," the Lord told Samuel. "I have chosen one of his sons to be the new king."

Samuel knew that Saul would be very angry if he heard there was to be a new king. He might try to harm Samuel. But Samuel obeyed God. He went to the house of Jesse. He did not tell Jesse why he had come.

Jesse and his sons welcomed Samuel. As each of the seven sons passed before Samuel, he wondered, "Is this the one the Lord has chosen?"

But each time God said, "No." Only Samuel could hear the voice of God.

At last Samuel asked Jesse, "Are all your sons here?"

"No," said Jesse. "My youngest son is only a boy. He is away, tending the sheep."

"Send for the boy," Samuel said. "I want to see him."

The boy came. His name was David. He was a handsome boy with bright, eager eyes. As Samuel looked at David, he heard the voice of the Lord.

The Lord said, "Arise and anoint him. This is the one I have chosen."

Samuel took the horn of oil and anointed David. But he did not tell anyone that David was to be the new king of Israel. Yet soon all Israel would know King David.

1 SAMUEL 17:45   *Then said David to the Philistine, Thou comest to me with a sword, and with a spear, and with a shield: but I come to thee in the name of the Lord of hosts, the God of the armies of Israel, whom thou hast defied.*

David and Goliath

MANY OF THE GREAT LEADERS of Israel had been shepherds. David was a shepherd boy, too. He tended his father's sheep as they grazed in the pastures and protected them from harm. When a lion or a bear tried to steal a lamb from the flock, David fought it off bravely.

Sometimes he was lonely with only the sheep for company. Then David sang songs to God about the things he knew and loved. He sang about green grass and still waters.

While David tended his sheep, there was war in the land. Again the people of Israel were fighting the Philistines. One day Jesse, the father of David, told him:

"Take this food to your brothers who are fighting with King Saul against the Philistines. Then come and tell me how they are."

David took the food to the army camp. King Saul and his soldiers were on the side of a mountain. Across the valley was another mountain. The Philistines were there.

Eagerly David looked among the soldiers in King Saul's camp. Where were his brothers? Just as he found them, a huge giant strode out from the Philistine army. The sun glinted on his bronze helmet and javelin and on his huge spear.

"Choose a man!" roared the giant to the soldiers of Israel. "Let him come out and fight me!"

"Who is that man?" David asked. "Will no one fight him?"

"That is Goliath," answered a soldier. "He is a mighty warrior. Who is big enough to fight him?"

"Let me fight him," said David.

The soldiers laughed. David's brothers were angry with him. They told him to go back to his sheep.

But King Saul did not laugh.

And David took his staff and put five smooth stones in his shepherd's bag and went out to fight Goliath.

All the soldiers watched as David went down the side of the mountain toward the Philistines.

How huge Goliath looked with his bronze helmet on his head and his sword and spear and bronze javelin!

How small David looked! He had no sword. He had only a slingshot and five stones in his shepherd's bag.

The giant Goliath roared with laughter.

"You are only a boy!" he shouted. "How can you fight me? You do not even have a sword."

But David was not afraid. He had fought a lion when it tried to steal a lamb from his flock of sheep. He had fought a bear. He could fight Goliath, too.

"I do not need a sword," he said. "God will help me."

When Goliath strode forward, David ran to meet him. He took a stone from his bag and put it in his slingshot. Then he whirled the slingshot and the stone flew through the air. It flew straight toward Goliath and struck the giant between the eyes.

With a mighty crash, Goliath fell to the ground!

All the soldiers were very still. Then the Philistines began to shake and tremble. Goliath was dead! They were afraid to stay and fight. They began to run away.

The soldiers of King Saul cheered and shouted and ran after the Philistines.

1 SAMUEL 18:1 *The soul of Jonathan was knit with the soul of David, and Jonathan loved him as his own soul.*

David and Jonathan

AFTER DAVID, the shepherd boy, killed the giant Goliath he was taken to the tent of King Saul. The king was greatly pleased with this brave boy who had conquered the mighty giant with only a slingshot.

King Saul invited David to live in the palace.

"You will stay with me now," King Saul told David.

Now David no longer tended his father's sheep. He lived in the palace of King Saul.

But David still sang songs. As he sang and played upon his harp, King Saul listened. He liked David's songs about the sheep and green pastures. He liked David's songs of praise to God. Often the king was ill and David's music comforted him and made him feel better.

King Saul had a son called Jonathan. And the first time David and Jonathan looked at each other, they liked each other and knew they would be friends.

Now David and Jonathan were often together. They talked together and laughed together. When Jonathan drew his bow and sent an arrow swiftly to its mark, David watched and was proud of his friend.

Jonathan gave David a fine robe to show how much he loved him. He gave him a sword and a bow, too. David and Jonathan promised to be friends always.

These were happy days for David. He and Jonathan were good friends. King Saul trusted him and sent him to lead soldiers in battle against the Philistines. David was a good soldier and won many battles.

One day when the soldiers were returning from battle, crowds of women came out to dance and sing before King Saul and David.

"Saul has killed thousands,
    And David has killed ten thousands," the women sang.

King Saul was very angry when he heard this song. He did not like the people to praise and admire David more than they admired him.

King Saul was jealous of David.

But David did not know this.

The next day King Saul was ill. David came to him and played on his harp and sang. But this time David's music did not comfort the jealous king. King Saul was filled with anger.

He threw his spear at David!

David dodged and the spear did not touch him.

Then King Saul threw another spear at David.

Again David dodged out of the way. The spear flew harmlessly through the air.

But still David did not know that King Saul was jealous of him and hated him. He did not know that the king really wanted to hurt him.

After this King Saul did not want David to be near him. He made him the leader of a thousand soldiers and sent him away to fight more battles.

David and his soldiers fought the enemy many times, and always they won the victory. The soldiers loved David. The people of Israel loved David, too.

But King Saul did not love David now. He grew more and more jealous of him.

King Saul did not know that Samuel had anointed David while he was still only a shepherd boy. He did not know God had chosen David to be the next king of Israel.

But he did know that the people loved David, and he was afraid. Saul was king. He wanted his son Jonathan to be king after him. He was afraid the people would want David to be their king.

Jonathan knew this, and it troubled him very much. He was not jealous of David. David was his friend, and he loved him.

At last David knew, too, that the king hated him.

One day, David and Jonathan walked out in a field where no one could hear them. They talked of King Saul.

"Let us try one more time," said Jonathan. "I will go back to the palace. I will find out if the king is still angry with you. Then I will come back and let you know. Hide here until I come."

David hid in the field. On the morning of the third day, David saw Jonathan coming. A little boy was with him, and Jonathan was carrying his bow and arrows.

"Run!" Jonathan said to the boy. "Find the arrows that I shoot and pick them up."

As the boy ran, Jonathan shot an arrow beyond him, toward the place where David was hiding.

"Hurry!" Jonathan called loudly. "Do not wait!"

Then David knew King Saul was still angry with him. Jonathan was not really calling to the little boy. He was telling David he must hurry and go away to be safe from the king.

After Jonathan sent the boy home, David came out from his hiding place. Sadly he and Jonathan said goodbye. They promised never to forget each other.

Then Jonathan went back to the palace, and David went to the hills to hide.

2 SAMUEL 7:8 *Thus saith the Lord of hosts, I took thee from the sheepcote, from following the sheep, to be ruler over my people, over Israel.*

David, the King

WHEN DAVID ran away from King Saul, he fled to the hills where there were caves where he could hide and live. Soon many brave men joined him. Some were soldiers who had fought for King Saul. Now they wanted to fight for David for all the people knew how bravely David had fought for his king and his country. They loved and trusted David.

Saul was very angry when he heard this. He tried to find David so he could kill him. David knew this, but he did not hate King Saul. Once Saul came into a cave where David and his men were hiding. Saul did not know David was there.

The men with David wanted to kill the king. But David would not let them.

Another time David stole at night into the camp where Saul's army was sleeping. King Saul was asleep, too. David looked down at the king.

A soldier with David wanted to kill Saul. But again David would not let this happen.

"Saul is the king," David said. "We must not harm him."

David took the spear and the water jar that were lying beside the sleeping king. Then he went to the top of the hill and called down to the camp. The soldiers awoke. King Saul awoke, too, and heard David's voice.

"I have the king's spear!" David called. "I have his water jar, too. I took them while you all slept."

Then King Saul knew that David could have killed him while he was asleep. But David had not harmed him. The king was sorry that he had hated David.

"Come back," Saul cried. "Come back to me, David."

David had proved to Saul that he was his friend. But David did not go back to King Saul. He knew that soon the king would change and hate him again.

David went away. This time Saul did not try to find him.

The Philistines began to fight Saul again. There was a great battle and Saul was killed. Prince Jonathan, David's friend, was killed, too. How sad David was when he heard this! He mourned for many days.

Now the people of Israel had no king. They came to David and asked him to be king. So the shepherd boy God had chosen to rule His people became king of Israel.

King David ruled for a long time. He tried to be a wise and good king and give justice to all his people. Sometimes he did wrong things, but then he was sorry and tried harder to do what was right.

David helped his country grow strong and powerful. He made Jerusalem the great city of his kingdom, and he built a wonderful palace there.

David brought the Ark with the Ten Commandments to the city, too. The people rejoiced and danced and sang.

But David still remembered his good friend Jonathan and how much he loved him.

One day David sat in his palace in Jerusalem.

"Is there anyone left of Saul's family?" asked King David. "I would like to be kind to him because I loved Jonathan."

Then a man came. He had been a servant to King Saul.

"Jonathan had a son," said the man. "He is still alive. He was a little boy when his father died in battle. His nurse was carrying him as she tried to run to a safe place. But she dropped him. Since then he has been lame."

"Where is he?" David asked eagerly. "Bring him to me."

The son of Jonathan was brought to the palace. He was a young man now. He was afraid at first as he limped up to King David and knelt before him.

David smiled at him.

"Do not be afraid," King David told him. "I will be kind to you because I loved your father Jonathan."

David gave Jonathan's son the land that had belonged to Saul. He kept him with him at the palace and he treated him like one of his own sons. King David had not forgotten his friend Jonathan.

All his life David loved God and sang songs of praise and prayer to Him just as he had done when he was a shepherd boy watching his sheep. Here are verses from some of the psalms he sang.

from PSALM 18:   *I will love Thee, O Lord, my strength.*
The Lord is my rock, and my fortress,
And my deliverer;
My God, my strength, in Whom I will trust.

from PSALM 19:   *The heavens declare the glory of God;*
And the firmament showeth His handywork.

from PSALM 24:   *The earth is the Lord's, and the fullness thereof;*
The world, and they that dwell therein.
For He hath founded it upon the seas,
And established it upon the floods.
Who shall ascend into the hill of the Lord?
Or who shall stand in His holy place?
He that hath clean hands, and a pure heart.

from PSALM 25:   *Show me Thy ways, O Lord;*
Teach me Thy paths.
Lead me in Thy truth, and teach me.

from PSALM 27:   *The Lord is my light and my salvation:*
Whom shall I fear?
The Lord is the strength of my life;
Of whom shall I be afraid?

Wait on the Lord:
Be of good courage,
And He shall strengthen thine heart.

from PSALM 28: *The Lord is my strength and my shield;*
My heart trusted in Him, and I am helped:
Therefore my heart greatly rejoiceth;
And with my song will I praise Him.

from PSALM 36: *How excellent is Thy loving-kindness, O God!*
Therefore the children of men put their trust
Under the shadow of Thy wings.

from PSALM 57: *I will praise Thee, O Lord, among the people:*
I will sing unto Thee among the nations.
For Thy mercy is great unto the heavens,
And Thy truth unto the clouds.

from PSALM 103: *Bless the Lord, O my soul:*
And all that is within me,
Bless His holy name.

1 KINGS 3:9   *Give therefore thy servant an understanding heart to judge thy people, that I may discern between good and bad: for who is able to judge this thy so great a people?*

Wise King Solomon

AFTER DAVID DIED, his son Solomon became king of Israel. Solomon wanted to be a good king, but he was very young. He knew that he needed God's help to rule over his people justly and wisely.

Solomon prayed to the Lord.

"I am very young," he told God. "I do not know enough to be a good king. Help me to understand when I judge my people. Help me to know what is good and what is bad."

God was pleased with Solomon. He was pleased that the new young king did not ask for anything for himself. He was pleased that Solomon asked only for wisdom to help his people and to be a good king.

God promised Solomon He would help him to rule wisely. He told Solomon too that He would also give him wealth and honor. He also promised Solomon that if he would remember God and live as God wanted him to live, then Solomon would live many years.

God did help Solomon and Solomon became known for his great wisdom. Many people came to him for help.

One day two women came to King Solomon. They had a baby with them.

"My Lord King," said one of the women. "This woman and I live in the same house. I had a baby, and she had a baby, too. We were alone in the house, and her baby died. In the night, she came and took away my baby."

The other woman said, "No, my baby is alive. This is my baby."

"No!" said the first woman. "It is my baby!"

King Solomon looked at the women and at the baby.

"Bring me a sword," he said.

When the sword came, Solomon said, "Divide the baby in two. Give half of the baby to each woman."

One of the women cried out.

"No! Do not kill the baby! Give it to her, but do not kill it. Let it live!"

But the other woman said, "Yes, divide the baby. Then neither of us will have it."

King Solomon smiled. He had tested the two women. Now he knew who was the mother of the child.

"Do not kill the baby," he said. "Give the child to the first woman. She loves the baby and wants it to live. She is its mother."

The news of Solomon's great wisdom traveled all through the world. People from far lands came to see him. They brought him wonderful gifts—silver and gold, spices and horses, and many other things.

And King Solomon built a splendid temple to God. He built it of huge stones and cedars of Lebanon and cypress wood. There were beautiful carvings on the walls and gold covered the floor. Inside the temple was an inner place and there was the altar to God. That was the most holy place of the temple.

For seven years, thousands of men worked to build the great temple. When it was finished, Solomon called the people together. The Ark with the Ten Commandments was put in the holy place.

Then Solomon and the people worshiped God together.

Elijah and the Prophets of Baal

ELIJAH WAS ONE of the greatest of God's prophets. He lived in a time when Israel was ruled by a wicked king and queen. They were called Ahab and Jezebel.

The king and queen did not follow the way of God. They led the people into the worship of idols and of strange gods.

Elijah was a good man. He loved God, and he wanted the people to love God and obey Him, too.

He went to King Ahab, and he told the king that God was going to punish him and the people because they did not follow God's way.

"There will be no dew in the land," Elijah warned the king. "There will be years when the rain does not fall."

King Ahab did not listen. And just as Elijah had warned the king, there came a time when there was no rain. Soon there was no food, too, for the plants needed water to grow. The people were hungry.

Then God told Elijah to go to King Ahab again.

Ahab was angry when he saw Elijah.

"Are you the one who has brought trouble to Israel?" King Ahab demanded.

Elijah was angry, too.

"I have not brought trouble to Israel," Elijah said. "It is you who have brought trouble to the people. You have led the people away from God. You have led them to worship the false god, Baal."

Then Elijah told King Ahab what God had commanded him to do.

"Gather the people together," Elijah said. "Send them to Mount Carmel. Send the prophets of Baal there, too."

The people of Israel gathered on Mount Carmel. The prophets of Baal gathered there, too.

Elijah stood before the people.

"You must choose," he told them. "You cannot worship God and Baal, too. If you believe in the Lord, you must follow His way. If you believe in Baal, follow Baal."

The people listened. They did not say one word.

Then Elijah told the people to bring two bulls.

"Let the prophets of Baal choose one of the bulls," he said. "I will take the other. We will cut up the bulls and put them on wood. But we will not light a fire. They will call to Baal. I will pray to God. We will see who answers."

"Good!" said all the people.

There were four hundred and fifty prophets of Baal. They chose a bull and cut it up and put it on wood. Then they called on Baal to light a fire. All morning and afternoon they called to Baal, but Baal did not answer.

Then Elijah called the people to come near him.

He took twelve stones and built an altar in the name of God. He made a trench around the altar and put the wood in place. He cut up a bull and put it on the wood.

96

Then Elijah told the people to fill four jars with water and pour the water on the bull. The people did this three times. The water ran around the altar. The trench filled with water, too.

Then Elijah prayed to God and God answered with fire!

The fire burned the bull and the wood and the stones and licked up the water in the trench.

Then the people knew that the Lord was God. The prophets of Baal were arrested. Not one escaped.

Soon the sky grew dark with clouds and wind. A great rain came to refresh the land of Israel.

NEHEMIAH 5:19   *Think upon me, my God, for good, according to all that I have done for this people.*

Nehemiah and the Wall

NEHEMIAH WAS ANOTHER of the wise and good men of the people of Israel. But he did not live in the land of Israel. There had been a war and Israel had lost it. After the war was over, many of the people had been carried away from their homes and made to live in strange lands.

Nehemiah lived in the land of Persia. There he served the king of Persia. The king's name was Artaxerxes. He liked and trusted Nehemiah so much that he made him his cupbearer.

In those days, wicked people sometimes put something in a king's cup of wine that would harm him. The cupbearer helped keep the king safe. When the king was thirsty, the cupbearer brought him a cup of wine to drink. But first he tasted the wine himself. Then he knew there was nothing in the wine to hurt the king.

Only a man the king trusted could be the cupbearer. Nehemiah was proud and happy to be cupbearer to the king.

But one day when Nehemiah brought the cup of wine to the king, his face was sad.

King Artaxerxes saw this.

"Why are you sad?" he asked Nehemiah.

"O king," Nehemiah said, "I have had visitors from my own country. They told me that the walls of our great city, Jerusalem, are broken down. Its gates are burned by fire."

His voice was filled with grief, for Nehemiah loved his own country and its great city, Jerusalem.

King Artaxerxes liked Nehemiah. He did not want him to be unhappy.

"How can I help you?" he asked.

"Let me go to Jerusalem," answered Nehemiah, "and build its walls again."

The king let Nehemiah go to Jerusalem. He gave him letters to give to the men who ruled the lands between Persia and Jerusalem. The letters told the men to help Nehemiah.

At last Nehemiah came to Jerusalem. At night he rode around the city. He rode from gate to gate and everywhere the walls were broken and had fallen down.

Then he called the people of Jerusalem together.

"Come," he said. "Let us all work together and build the walls of Jerusalem again. Then we can be proud again of our city."

The people had been too sad to try to rebuild the walls alone. But now as they listened, they began to hope again.

"Let us rise up and build," they said bravely.

So the people began to work. From every part of the city, the people came to help rebuild the wall. They built the gates again, too, and set the doors in the gates and put on the bolts and bars.

For many days they worked together. At last the great wall was done. The wall again rose firmly around Jerusalem.

How the people rejoiced!

But Nehemiah called the people together again. As they stood in the city square under the blue sky, he had the word of God read to all the people. And the people listened and promised to try again to live as God wanted them to live. They promised again to keep God's commandments.

Then there was a great celebration and the people gave thanks to God for all His goodness. They thanked God for helping them build a strong wall around their city again and there was singing and music and laughter.

DANIEL 6:27   *He delivereth and rescueth, and he worketh signs and wonders in heaven and in earth, who hath delivered Daniel from the power of the lions.*

Daniel in the Lion's Den

LONG AGO IN JERUSALEM, there was a boy named Daniel. At that time Nebuchadnezzar, King of Babylon, made war on Jerusalem and conquered the city.

Then the king commanded, "Bring me boys of the noble houses of Israel. Bring me only boys who are handsome and strong and quick to learn. We will take them to Babylon with us."

Daniel was a strong boy and handsome. His eyes were bright with curiosity and he was eager to learn and understand all he saw. So he was one of the boys who was carried away to Babylon.

There Daniel and the other boys from Israel lived in the palace of the king. They were taught the language of the people of Babylon and many other things the king wanted them to know.

101

"Take good care of these boys," King Nebuchadnezzar commanded. "Give them food from my own table. Do this for three years. Then bring them before me so I may see who is the strongest and wisest of them."

But Daniel did not want to eat the rich food or drink the wine from the king's own table. He knew that God had told the people of Israel to eat certain kinds of food and that there were certain foods they must not eat.

Daniel told this to the man whom the king had put in charge of the boys from Israel.

"Let me eat vegetables and drink water," Daniel said to the man. "Do not make me eat the king's food."

The man liked Daniel and wanted to please him. But he was afraid to disobey the king.

"What will the king say," the man asked, "if you are brought before him and the boys who have eaten his food are stronger than you are? He will blame me and my life will be in danger."

"Let me try my own food for just ten days," Daniel said. "Then see who is stronger."

The man agreed. Daniel ate vegetables and drank water. At the end of ten days, he was even stronger than the boys who had eaten the king's rich food!

So Daniel went on eating vegetables and drinking water and he was happy because he could obey God's command.

At the end of three years, all the boys from Israel were brought before King Nebuchadnezzar. The king looked at all the boys carefully to see which boys were strongest and healthiest. He asked each boy many questions.

Daniel stood straight and strong and handsome as he answered all the king's questions. He answered them so well that the king made him one of his wise men.

Daniel gave the king good advice. He told him the meaning of his dreams. The king trusted Daniel.

New kings ruled Babylon and Daniel gave them advice, too.

But always Daniel prayed to God and asked His help.

When King Darius ruled Babylon, he trusted Daniel so much that other men became jealous of Daniel. They wanted him killed, and they thought up a wicked plan.

They went to the king and asked him to make a new law. This law said that for thirty days, no man should ask anybody but the king for help—not even God.

The men knew that Daniel asked God for help every day. They knew he would not stop praying to God even if the king commanded it.

The king signed the new law. Daniel was sad when he heard this. But he went home and prayed to God anyway.

Then the men told the king. The king was filled with sorrow. He knew now that he had signed a bad law. But it was the law and even the king could not help Daniel.

The king ordered that Daniel be put in a den of lions.

"May your God help you now!" he said to Daniel, and he had a stone brought and put across the opening of the den so Daniel could not get out.

Then the king set his own seal on the stone so no one would dare move it.

He left Daniel in the den of lions. He went back sadly to his palace. He was so sad that he would not eat or sleep. All night he wondered what had happened to Daniel and his heart was full of fear and grief.

When dawn came, the king hurried to the den of lions.

The king called to Daniel, "O Daniel, has your God been able to save you from the lions?"

Then Daniel called, "My God sent His angel and shut the lions' mouths. They have not hurt me."

How happy the king was then! He had Daniel taken from the lion's den. He put the wicked men who had plotted against Daniel in the den instead.

Daniel had trusted God and God had saved him. And King Darius praised the God of Israel to all the people.

Stories from The New Testament

LUKE 2:11   *For unto you is born this day in the city of David a Saviour, which is Christ the Lord.*

Jesus Is Born

FOR MANY, many years the people of Israel had a wonderful dream. They dreamed that someday a king would come to rule over them. This king would be chosen by God. He would come and set the people free. He would bring peace to all people.

Sometimes it was hard to hold on to this dream. There were Roman soldiers in the streets. A Roman governor ruled the land of Israel.

There was a girl who believed in the dream and trusted in God. Her name was Mary.

One day Mary sat at the window in her room. Soon she would be married to Joseph. He was a carpenter and he was good and kind. Mary was happy as she thought about her wedding and of the goodness of God.

Suddenly an angel in a shining robe appeared to Mary. He brought her wonderful news.

"God is sending you a son," the angel told her. "His name will be Jesus. He will be called the Son of God, and He will rule over all people."

After the angel had gone, Mary sat and wondered at what he had told her. But she trusted in God. She wanted to do what God wanted her to do.

Mary and Joseph were married, and one day an order came from the king. Each man must go back to the town where he was born to be counted and taxed.

Joseph had been born in Bethlehem. He lifted Mary onto a small donkey, and they started on their way. It was a long way to Bethlehem. Many people were on the road.

At last they came to Bethlehem. How glad Mary was to see the lights of the inn through the dark night! She was very tired, for her Baby was to be born soon.

But the inn was crowded. There was no room for Mary and Joseph.

There was a stable in back of the inn. Joseph led Mary into it. He made a bed of soft, clean straw for her, and there the Child was born. How little He was and sweet! As Mary smiled, she saw a single star shining brightly over the stable.

Mary saw the bright star shining. There were others who saw that bright shining star, too.

That night in the fields outside the little town of Bethlehem, shepherds were watching their sheep.

Suddenly the night sky all around them was filled with a bright shining light, and an angel of the Lord came before them.

The shepherds trembled and were much afraid. What wonder was this?

But the angel said, "Do not be afraid. I bring you news of great joy to all people. A Child has been born in Bethlehem, a Saviour who is Christ, the Lord. He lies in a stable there."

Then the air was filled with a joyful singing as if all the angels in heaven were singing the glad news together.

"*Glory!*" sang the angels. "*Glory! Glory to God in the Highest! And on earth peace, good will to men!*"

Then the angels were gone. The night was dark again.

The shepherds and their sheep were alone on the hill. How still the night was all around them!

"Come," said one shepherd and then another and another. "Let us go to Bethlehem and see this Baby that the angel told us about."

And the shepherds left the fields and went quickly to the little town of Bethlehem. They saw the bright star shining over the stable.

Very quietly, they went into the stable. How peaceful it was! A cow mooed softly. And there were Mary and Joseph. There was the Child lying in His manger cradle.

A great joy filled the shepherds. They knelt before the Child and thanked God for sending Him. One shepherd was carrying a lamb, and it bleated softly.

The Child opened His eyes and smiled.

Then the shepherds went away to tell what they had seen and heard. And all who listened to them wondered about the story the shepherds told. What did it mean? Was the dream really coming true? Was the King born who would bring peace to all people?

MATTHEW 2:11 *And when they were come into the house, they saw the young child with Mary his mother, and fell down, and worshipped him: and when they had opened their treasures, they presented unto him gifts; gold, and frankincense, and myrrh.*

The Wise Men and the Star

THE SHEPHERDS saw the bright new star in the sky. Far away in the East, certain Wise Men saw the bright star shining, too. They knew something wonderful had happened.

They knew that a Baby had been born who was to be King of the Jews.

"Let us follow the star until we find the Child," they said, and they took gifts and got on their camels and began their journey. At last they came to Jerusalem.

"Where is He that is born King of the Jews?" the Wise Men asked the people. "We have seen His star in the East, and we have come to worship Him."

Now at that time King Herod ruled the Jews under the Roman governor. As Herod sat in his palace, he heard of the coming of the Wise Men. He heard of the questions they asked, and he was afraid. Where was this new King? Would He take away King Herod's throne?

King Herod sent for the Wise Men.

"Go to Bethlehem," he told them. "Find the new-born King. Then come and tell me where He is, and I will go and worship Him, too."

The Wise Men left King Herod and journeyed on. They followed the bright new star shining in the sky. It led them to the town of Bethlehem. There they saw the star shining above a little house.

With great joy the Wise Men got off their camels and went into the house. And there was Mary with the Child Jesus.

Joyfully the Wise Men knelt and worshiped the Child and gave Him the splendid gifts they had brought.

Then the Wise Men traveled on, but God sent a dream to warn them not to go back to King Herod. The Wise Men went back to their own country by another way.

The Flight into Egypt

SOON AFTER the Wise Men left, Joseph had a dream. In the dream, an angel of the Lord came to him.

"Get up," the angel told Joseph. "Take the Baby and His mother and go away from here quickly. Go to Egypt and stay there until I tell you it is safe to come back. For King Herod will look for the Child to kill Him."

Joseph woke. The darkness of night was all around him. But Joseph did not wait. God had warned him in a dream, and he must obey God. Quickly, he got up.

He woke Mary.

"Get up," Joseph whispered to her. "Get up quickly. We must go away from here before King Herod finds us. We must not let him find us. We must not let him find the Child!"

Can you imagine how Mary and Joseph hurried and stumbled in the darkness as they gathered their things together for their journey?

Soon they were ready. The Baby was in Mary's arms. She held Him close.

"Come," Joseph said, and they stole into the night. He lifted Mary to the donkey's back. They were on their way!

It was a long journey to Egypt. On and on they traveled. Sometimes they stopped to rest for a little while, but soon they hurried on again. At last they reached Egypt and were safe.

They stayed in Egypt until King Herod died. Then an angel of the Lord came to Joseph in a dream again and told him it was safe to go back to Israel. And Joseph took Mary and the Child back to Nazareth, his old home.

Luke 2:49 *How is it that ye sought me? Wist ye not that I must be about my Father's business?*

The Boy Jesus

THE BOY JESUS grew up in the town of Nazareth. Can you imagine what it was like to be a boy long ago in Nazareth? The town lay on a hill. When you looked down, you could see the busy highways where soldiers and traders traveled to far places.

Did the Boy Jesus look down on the highways? What did He think and wonder? But there was little time for wonder. There was much for Him to learn and do.

Joseph had a carpenter shop in Nazareth. When Jesus was a little boy, He learned to help Joseph in the shop. He ran errands. He swept up the wood shavings. Later He learned how to use a hammer and a saw. He learned how to make things of wood.

He helped Mary, His mother, too. He learned to read and write. And as He helped and learned, the Boy grew strong and gentle and wise.

Then Jesus was twelve years old.

Each year Mary and Joseph went to Jerusalem, the Holy City, for the feast of the Passover.

This year Mary said to Jesus, "You are old enough now, my Son. You will come with us to Jerusalem."

It was a long way to Jerusalem. Many relatives and friends went with Mary and Joseph and Jesus as they set out on the journey. At last they came to the city gates.

The city was crowded. From all parts of the country, people had come to celebrate the Passover feast. The feast lasted a week. Then Mary and Joseph started out on the long journey home. Their friends and relatives went with them.

At the end of the first day of the journey, Mary looked for Jesus. But where was He? Mary and Joseph went from friend to friend, from relative to relative.

"Have you seen Jesus?" they asked. "We thought He was with you."

They did not find Jesus. Where was the Boy? Was He lost in the crowded city of Jerusalem? Anxiously Mary and Joseph hurried back to the city.

For three days they looked for Jesus in the city streets. At last they went to the temple. There were the wise men, the teachers of the law. And there was the Boy Jesus! He was asking the wise men questions. He was answering their questions, too. All who listened were filled with wonder.

How surprised Mary and Joseph were!

Mary went to Jesus. "My Son," she said, "why did you do this to us? Your father and I were afraid harm had come to you. We have looked for you everywhere."

But Jesus answered, "Did you not know that I would be here in the temple, about my Father's business?"

Then He went home with them to Nazareth. But Mary remembered His words and thought of them often.

LUKE 3:22 *Thou art my beloved Son; in thee I am well pleased.*

Jesus and John the Baptist

THE BOY JESUS went home to Nazareth. As the years went by, He grew tall. He grew in wisdom, too, and all who knew Him loved Him. He was a man now, and He knew it was time for Him to leave home. It was time for Him to go among the people and tell them of God and how God wanted them to live.

At that time another young man came out of the wilderness. He wore a robe made of camel's hair, fastened with a leather belt. He ate only locusts and wild honey. This man was named John.

John went from place to place around Jordan and told the people about God and His promises.

"Come and tell God you are sorry for the wrong things you have done," John said to the people.

Many people came to listen to him.

"What shall we do?" they asked John. "How can we show God we are sorry?"

"Share with each other," John told them. "Help each other and try to do right."

Many people promised John they would try to live as God wanted them to live.

Then they were washed in the waters of the river Jordan. This was how they showed that they wanted to wash away all the wrong things they had done and begin a new life.

This was called baptism and sometimes John was called John the Baptist.

One day Jesus came to the river. He saw John baptizing the people. He asked John to baptize Him, too.

"You do not need me to baptize you," John told Him. "I need to be baptized by you."

But when Jesus asked him again, John baptized Jesus. And as Jesus rose from the river, a dove lit on Him, and a voice came from heaven, saying:

"Thou art my beloved Son; in thee I am well pleased."

After this Jesus went alone into the wilderness to think and pray.

For forty days, Jesus stayed in the wilderness. He ate no food. He fasted and thought of the work He must do. Jesus knew that the work would be hard and full of danger. Can you imagine that sometimes He was tempted not to do this dangerous work?

But Jesus fought the temptation. He prayed to God for help. He asked God to make Him strong and brave and to help Him do His work well.

While Jesus was in the wilderness, John the Baptist went on with his work. John went on preaching to the people, telling them of God and how He wanted them to live. The king heard about John and his preaching. The king sent soldiers to arrest John and put him in prison.

After forty days Jesus came out of the wilderness. He was told that John was in prison. Now it was time for Jesus to begin His work.

Jesus went to Galilee. He began the work God had sent Him to do.

MATTHEW 4:19   *Follow me,
and I will make you fishers of
men.*

Jesus Finds His Helpers

JESUS KNEW that He would need men to help Him in His
work. Where could He find them? One day as Jesus walked
by the Sea of Galilee, He saw two fishermen throwing their
nets into the sea to catch fish.

These two fishermen were brothers. Jesus knew that they
had helped John the Baptist in his work.

Jesus stood on the shore and watched the two brothers
as they fished.

Then He called to them.

"Follow me," He said. "I will make you fishers of men."

The two brothers looked at Him in surprise. How could they fish for men?

Jesus smiled. "I will teach you to gather men as you gather your fish," he said. "I will show you how to call them to come and listen and learn. We will work together to teach people how God wants them to live."

The two brothers dropped their fishing nets. They went with Jesus happily.

One of these brothers was named Simon, but Jesus called him Peter, which means the Rock. Peter was to be one of the best friends and helpers of Jesus. The other brother was called Andrew.

As they went along the shore of the sea, Jesus saw a fishing boat. In the ship, two men sat mending their nets.

Jesus called to them to come and help Him in His work, and they, too, went with Jesus.

These two fishermen were also brothers and their names were James and John.

As Jesus went on with His work, more and more people heard about Him. He found more men to help Him tell the people about God and how God wanted people to love one another.

Twelve of these men became Jesus's best friends and helpers. They are called His disciples or apostles.

LUKE 10:37b *Then said Jesus unto him, Go, and do thou likewise.*

The Story of the Good Samaritan

SOMETIMES JESUS told stories to help teach the people how God wanted them to live. This is one of the stories that Jesus told.

One day a man was hurrying along the road that led from Jerusalem to Jericho. The road twisted through woods on the rocky hillside. There were caves in the rocks, and the man was afraid. Soon it would be dark and robbers lived in the caves!

Just as the man passed a cave, some robbers jumped out at him. They tore off his robe and took away his money. Then they hurt him and left him alone on the road.

It grew darker and darker, but the man was too hurt to move. As he lay there, a priest came down the road.

"Help me!" the man begged.

But the priest was frightened, too. He did not stop to help the man. He hurried away on the other side of the lonely dark road.

After awhile, another man came down the road. He was a good man, but he was frightened, too. He saw the hurt man, but he did not stop to help. He, too, hurried on his way.

Then a stranger rode down the road on a donkey. He did not live in the same country as the hurt man. He lived in a land called Samaria, so he was called a Samaritan.

But the stranger saw the hurt man and was sorry for him. He stopped and got off his donkey. His hands were gentle as he put medicine on the hurt man and bandaged him.

Then he lifted the hurt man on to his own donkey and carefully led him to an inn.

All night the stranger took care of the hurt man. And in the morning, he gave money to the innkeeper.

"Take care of this poor hurt man," said the stranger. "If you spend more than this money, I will pay you when I come this way again."

When Jesus finished telling this story, He asked, "Which of these three men was a good neighbor?"

"The man who stopped and helped," said a man from the listening crowd.

"Yes," said Jesus. "And God wants us all to help each other and be good neighbors, too."

And He
opened His mouth,
and taught them,
saying—

One morning Jesus stood on a mountain. He looked down at the crowds of people who had followed Him. He called His disciples up to Him. This is what He taught them there.

Blessed are the poor in spirit:
    for theirs is the kingdom of heaven.

Blessed are they that mourn:
    for they shall be comforted.

Blessed are the meek:
    for they shall inherit the earth.

Blessed are they which do hunger and thirst after righteousness:
    for they shall be filled.

Blessed are the merciful:
    for they shall obtain mercy.

Blessed are the pure in heart:
    for they shall see God.

Blessed are the peacemakers:
    for they shall be called the children of God.

Blessed are they which are persecuted for righteousness' sake:
    for theirs is the kingdom of heaven.

Blessed are ye,
    when men shall revile you, and persecute you,
    and shall say all manner of evil against you falsely,
    for my sake.

Rejoice, and be exceeding glad:
    for great is your reward in heaven:
    for so persecuted they the prophets which were before you.

—MATTHEW 5:2-12

LUKE 9:16 *Then he took the five loaves and the two fishes, and looking up to heaven, he blessed them, and brake, and gave to the disciples to set before the multitude.*

Jesus Feeds the People

NOW MANY PEOPLE had heard of Jesus and crowds followed Him wherever he went. One day the people followed Him to a lonely place beside the sea.

Jesus welcomed the people and spoke to them of God. He healed many who were ill.

The sun climbed high in the sky. The shadows grew long. Soon darkness would come, but still the people stayed and listened to Jesus.

The disciples saw this. They grew troubled, and they came to Jesus.

"Send the people away now," they said. "Soon it will be night. The people are growing hungry. Tell them to go and find food and a place to rest for the night. For we are in a lonely place, and we have no food to give them."

"Give them something to eat," Jesus told His disciples.

But the disciples answered, "We have only five loaves of bread and two fishes. How can we feed all these people? We would have to go and buy food."

Jesus looked at the crowd. There were many, many people around Him.

He said to His disciples:

"Ask the people to sit down in groups of fifty."

The disciples looked again at the five loaves of bread. They looked at the two fishes. Then they looked at the many, many people who crowded around Jesus, listening to Him.

The disciples looked at Jesus in wonder and surprise. How could five loaves of bread and two fishes feed all these people?

But the disciples asked no more questions. They did as Jesus had told them to do. They told the people to sit down in groups of fifty.

Then Jesus took the five loaves of bread and the two fishes. He looked to heaven and blessed the food and broke it into small pieces. Jesus gave the food to the disciples, and they passed among the crowd, giving the food to the waiting people.

When everyone had had enough to eat, the disciples gathered what was left in twelve baskets. Then as night came, Jesus sent the people away to find places to rest for the night.

MATTHEW 14:27 *But straight-away Jesus spake unto them, saying, Be of good cheer; it is I; be not afraid.*

Jesus Walks on the Stormy Waters

AFTER the huge crowd of people had been fed, Jesus sent His disciples away.

"Take a boat," He told them, "and cross to the other side. I will come later."

Then Jesus waited for the people to go away. Slowly, one by one and in little groups, all the people went away.

When Jesus was alone at last, He was tired. He went up into the hills to pray to God for strength to do the work God wanted Him to do.

Evening came. Alone on the hill, Jesus looked down at the sea. He saw the boat with His disciples in it. The boat was far out on the sea. A strong wind was blowing and the boat rocked on the waves.

Jesus came down from the hills. When He reached the shore, the wind was blowing stronger and stronger. The boat was tossing on the stormy sea.

Jesus began to walk out on the stormy waters.

When His disciples saw Him, they were afraid. They did not know it was Jesus. They thought He was a spirit, and they cried out in fear.

Jesus saw that they were afraid.

"Do not be afraid!" He called out to them. "It is I. There is nothing to fear!"

When the disciples heard His voice, they knew it was Jesus. But how could he walk on the stormy sea?

"Lord!" called out Peter. "If it is really you, tell me to come to you on the water."

And Jesus said, "Come to me."

Then Peter stepped out of the boat. He stepped out on the stormy waves. He began to walk toward Jesus.

But when Peter saw the wind-tossed waves and felt the strong wind blowing him, too, Peter was afraid. He began to sink.

"Lord!" Peter called. "Save me!"

At once Jesus stretched out His hand. He caught Peter. "Why were you afraid?" Jesus asked. "Why did you doubt me?"

Together, Jesus and Peter came to the boat and got into it. And the wind stopped blowing. The waters were still. The people in the boat came to Jesus and worshipped Him.

LUKE 17:19 *And he said unto him, Arise, go thy way: thy faith hath made thee whole.*

Jesus Heals the Lepers

JESUS HEALED many people who were sick. One of the most terrible sicknesses of the people of that time was called leprosy. It was so bad a sickness that those who had it could not live with other people. They had to live by themselves outside the towns.

One day as Jesus came close to a town, ten of these sick men called lepers came to meet Him. They had heard that Jesus had helped other sick people. They wanted Jesus to help them, too.

The men did not come close to Jesus. They stood a little way off and called, "Master, have mercy on us!"

They wanted Jesus to heal them as He had healed other sick people.

Jesus was filled with pity as He looked at them.

"Go and show yourselves to the priests," he told them.

That was His way of saying He would help them. For it was the law at that time that the priests decided when a man was cured of leprosy and could go home to his family.

At once the ten men began to run toward the priests. As they ran, they were cured of their sickness.

One of the men stopped. He looked at himself. He saw he was well again. Jesus had made him well!

The man turned back. He cried out his praise of the wonderful goodness of God. Then he knelt at the feet of Jesus and thanked Him.

This man was a Samaritan, a stranger from another land.

Jesus was sad. Ten men had had a terrible sickness. Ten men had been healed of their sickness. Where were the other nine men? Only this stranger had come back to thank God and praise Him.

Then Jesus spoke to the man. "Rise and go your way," Jesus said. "Your faith has made you well again."

LUKE 21:3 *And he said, Of a truth I say unto you, that this poor widow hath cast in more than they all.*

The Widow's Gift

As MORE and more people listened to Jesus, the leaders of the people wanted to meet Jesus, too. They wanted to talk with Him in places where people would see them with Jesus. They wanted to show the people how much they knew about the law of the church and how good they were.

One day Jesus stood at the door of the temple. He saw rich men come in and put money in the offering boxes. He saw them walk out proudly because they had given many coins.

As Jesus watched, another rich man came to the offering box. He, too, put a rich gift of money in the box and smiled proudly at the people watching.

Then Jesus saw a poor widow come to the box. She was dressed in shabby clothes. Her hands were rough from hard work. She dropped a copper coin into the box. Then she carefully dropped another copper coin into the box.

Jesus turned to His disciples who were near Him.

"This woman gave only two copper coins," He said. "But truly I tell you that she gave more than all the rich men gave. They have much wealth, and they gave some of what they had. But this poor widow gave all she had."

And the people listened as Jesus spoke and thought of the words He had spoken and marveled at His wisdom.

LUKE 19:5 *And when Jesus came to the place, he looked up, and saw him, and said unto him, Zacchaeus, make haste, and come down; for today I must abide at thy house.*

Zacchaeus Climbs a Tree

WHEREVER JESUS went now, crowds came to see and listen to Him. One day as He was passing through the city of Jericho, the people heard He was there. A great crowd gathered to see Him. Shouts rang out that He had come.

In the crowd was a man called Zacchaeus. He collected taxes from the people, and he kept some of the tax money for himself. This made him a very rich man. But because he collected the tax money people did not like him, and he had no friends.

Zacchaeus wanted to see Jesus and hear His words.

But Zacchaeus was a very small man. He could not see over the heads of the crowd. He tried to jump high but still he could not see Jesus. Then he tried to push through the crowd, but too many people were in the way. Zacchaeus almost gave up, but then he had an idea.

He knew where Jesus would pass next. Zacchaeus left the crowd and ran to the place. Down the road he saw a sycamore tree.

Zacchaeus ran to the tree. He climbed up into the branches of the tree!

As Zacchaeus perched in the tree, he looked down the road. Soon he saw Jesus coming toward him. The crowd was following Jesus.

Jesus looked up. He saw Zacchaeus.

"Zacchaeus!" Jesus called. "Come down quickly! For I must stay at your house today."

Joyfully Zacchaeus scrambled down from the tree as fast as he could. He told Jesus how happy he was to see Him and have Him come to his home.

A murmur of surprise came from the crowd. And when they saw Jesus go home with Zacchaeus, they whispered to each other.

"Zacchaeus is not a good man," they whispered. "He takes our money to make himself rich. Why does Jesus go to his house?"

Zacchaeus heard the whispers. He stood as tall as he could.

"Behold, Lord," he said to Jesus, "I give half of my money to the poor. And if I have taken anything from any man that I should not take, I will give back four times as much."

All the crowd listened. They listened, too, as Jesus answered.

"This day," Jesus said to Zacchaeus, "salvation has come to this house."

Zacchaeus was not a small man in the eyes of the Lord.

Let Little Children Come to Me

WHEN JESUS spoke, people came from all around to hear Him. Rich men and poor men came. Boys and girls came, too. Women brought their little children to see Jesus and to listen to His words.

One day as Jesus was telling the people about God and how God wanted them to live, there was a great crowd around Him. Many rich and important men were in the crowd. The friends and helpers of Jesus, His disciples, were pleased with this. They wanted important men to hear what Jesus had to say.

At the edge of the crowd were many women. Some had babies in their arms. Others held little boys and girls by the hand. Older boys and girls had come with their mothers, too.

The women and children tried to press through the huge crowd. The mothers wanted to come close to Jesus. They wanted Jesus to touch their children and bless them.

But the disciples saw them.
They were not pleased. They
did not think the women and
children should come to see
Jesus when He was busy with
important men.

As the women with their
babies and the boys and girls
tried to come close to Jesus,
the disciples held them back.

"Go away," they told the
women and children. "Jesus
is too busy to see you now."

How sad the women and
the children were!

Slowly the women began to turn away. But the little children held back. They tugged at their mothers' hands. They did not want to go away.

The boys and girls stood still, too. They wanted to come close to Jesus. He was their friend. Often He told them wonderful stories.

"Go home," the disciples told the children.

Just then, Jesus looked up. He saw what His disciples were doing. He saw the unhappy children.

Jesus turned from the important men around Him. He held out His arms to the children.

"Let the children come to me," Jesus said. "Do not try to stop them."

With a happy shout, the children ran to Jesus! They pressed against His knees. They leaned against Him and stroked His robe.

The mothers came close, too, with their babies. A baby reached out its hands. Jesus took the baby on His lap.

Jesus smiled at the children. He put His hand on every child. He blessed them all.

"Let little children come to me," Jesus said. "Do not try to stop them. For of such is the kingdom of heaven."

Jesus was the friend of all children.

LUKE 19:38 *Saying, Blessed be the King that cometh in the name of the Lord: peace in heaven, and glory in the highest.*

Palm Sunday

NOW JESUS knew that it was time for Him to go again to the city of Jerusalem. He knew that He would face danger there for some people in the city were afraid of Him. They saw the way the people came to listen to Him. They saw that the people believed Him. They were afraid of His power over the people.

But Jesus knew that God wanted Him to face this danger so He started on the journey.

As Jesus drew near a village east of Jerusalem on the Mount of Olives, He called two of His disciples to Him.

"Go into the village," He told them. "You will see a donkey and·her colt tied there. It will be a colt that has never had a rider. Untie the colt and bring it to me."

The disciples looked at Jesus in wonder.

Jesus said, "If anyone asks you why you are untying the colt, say that the Lord needs it."

The disciples went to the village. They found the colt and brought it to Jesus. They spread their robes on the colt to make a riding pad and Jesus sat on it. Then He rode down the slope of the Mount of Olives. His disciples went with Him.

Crowds of people followed Jesus, too. Many threw robes and other garments on the road for Him to ride over. Some cut branches from the palm trees and scattered the branches on the road before Him, too.

As Jesus rode toward Jerusalem, the disciples and the crowd sang songs of praise to God for all Jesus had done.

They sang, *"Blessed be the King who comes in the name of the Lord! Peace in heaven and glory in the highest!"*

Many people came out to watch. Some did not like Jesus and His preaching. They asked Him to stop the singing.

Jesus would not do this. "If they stopped singing," He said, "even the stones would cry out."

When Jesus reached Jerusalem, He went into the temple. He preached, and many people came to hear Him. This made the priests and rulers of the city angry. But the people went on listening to Jesus.

LUKE 22:18   *For I say unto you, I will not drink of the fruit of the vine, until the kingdom of God shall come.*

The Last Supper

IT WAS almost time again for the Passover feast. Again the people of Israel were making ready to eat unleavened bread and bitter herbs and give thanks to God for bringing them out of slavery in Egypt.

All over the city of Jerusalem, people were busy, making ready for the Passover feast. Many people from the little country villages had come to Jerusalem to stay for the feast. They went about the crowded city streets looking for rooms for their families. People thronged to the market place, too. They bought bitter herbs. They bought figs and honey, olives and red pomegranates, and other good things to eat, too.

But some people in the city were making other plans. The priests and leaders of the city were afraid of Jesus and His power over the people. They wanted to arrest Him and kill Him.

"But when can we do it?" asked these priests and leaders of the city. "We cannot do it during the Passover feast, for the people would be angry and rise against us."

152

As the priests planned and plotted, a man came to them. This man was one of the twelve disciples Jesus had chosen. His name was Judas Iscariot.

"What will you give me if I help you arrest Jesus?" Judas asked.

The priests gave Judas thirty pieces of silver, and he promised to betray Jesus.

The day of the Passover feast came. Jesus and His friends were in the village of Bethany, outside of the city of Jerusalem.

Jesus spoke to two of His disciples.

"Peter and John," He said, "I want you to go and make the Passover feast ready. We will eat it together."

"Where do you want to eat it?" asked Peter and John.

"Go into the city," Jesus told them. "There you will see a man carrying a pitcher of water. Follow him home and ask the owner of the house if he has a room where the Teacher and His twelve friends may eat the Passover feast."

Peter and John listened carefully.

Jesus said, "The man will lead you upstairs. There you will find a large, furnished room. Prepare the Passover feast there."

Peter and John went to the city of Jerusalem. They saw many men in its streets. Where was the man they wanted?

153

Peter and John looked up and down the crowded streets of the city. Then, just as Jesus had told them, they saw a man carrying a pitcher of water. They followed him to his home and spoke to the owner of the house. He led them up a stairway to a large, furnished room.

"This is the room Jesus told us about," said Peter and John. Then they went out into the city streets again and bought food for the Passover feast.

The sun went down. Evening came. It was time for the Passover feast to begin. The table was laid. The feast was ready.

Jesus sat at the supper table. His twelve disciples sat at the table with Him.

Jesus was sad. He knew that this was the last supper He would eat with His disciples. He told them this, and they were sad, too. They loved Jesus, and now they knew that He would be taken from them.

Jesus took a cup of wine and blessed it.

"Take this," He said. "Share it with each other."

Then He took bread and broke it and gave it to them.

"Take and eat this," He said. "It is my body."

Then He took another cup of wine and said, "Drink this. This is my blood of the new testament, which shall be shed for many."

Then Jesus looked at His twelve disciples.

"One of you," He said sadly, "will not be true to me. Truly, I say to you, one of you will betray me."

The disciples looked at each other. How sad they were! They loved Jesus. How could one of them betray Him?

"Who is it?" they all asked. "Which one of us is it?"

Jesus knew that soon they would all know the answer. "Love one another," He said. "Share with each other."

And He went to the Mount of Olives, and His disciples followed Him.

MATTHEW 26:39   *O my Father, if it be possible, let this cup pass from me: nevertheless not as I will, but as thou wilt.*

Jesus in the Garden

THERE WAS a garden on the Mount of Olives. It was called Gethsemane and olive trees grew there. As Jesus and His disciples walked there, it was dark and quiet. The wind murmured softly in the leaves overhead.

Jesus was sad. He knew what was going to happen soon.

"Stay here," He said to Peter and two other disciples. "Watch with me. I am going under the trees to pray."

Jesus went alone under the dark trees. His heart was heavy with sorrow as He knelt and prayed.

He knew that soon a time of great suffering would come. But it was hard for even Jesus to face. Did God really want Jesus to face it? Jesus wanted to do whatever God wanted Him to do.

"My Father," Jesus prayed, "if you are willing, take this cup away from me. But let your will, not mine, be done."

Then Jesus went back to His three disciples. They had fallen asleep on the grass, for they were very tired and troubled.

Sadly Jesus woke them.

"Could you not stay awake one hour and watch with me?" He asked them. "Stay awake and watch now. Pray that you will not be tempted."

Again Jesus went away under the dark trees and prayed. When He came back, the three disciples were sleeping again.

This time Jesus did not wake them. For the third time, He went away and prayed.

Then again He came back to His disciples. Again they were sleeping. Jesus woke them.

"The time has come," He told them. "Let us go."

For Jesus could see torches shining brightly through the branches of the olive trees. He could see the crowd of men carrying the torches. There were soldiers with swords. There were men with clubs, too.

Judas was at the head of the crowd.

As the crowd came near, Judas went to Jesus. He kissed Jesus on the cheek. This was how Judas told the soldiers that this was Jesus.

Then the soldiers arrested Jesus and took Him away.

LUKE 23:46 *And when Jesus had cried with a loud voice, he said, Father, into thy hands I commend my spirit.*

The Trial and the Crucifixion

As SOON as the sun rose, the chief priests and leaders came together. They had Jesus brought before them.

Then they asked Him many questions. They called in men to tell of wrong things Jesus had done or said.

Some men came and lied about Jesus.

Then the high priest stood up.

"Did these men tell the truth?" he asked Jesus. "How do you answer them?"

Jesus did not say a word. He would not answer the high priest.

Then the high priest said, "Are you the Christ? Tell us."

Then Jesus said, "If I tell you, you will not believe me. You will not let me go. But hereafter the Son of man shall sit on the right hand of the power of God."

160

Then the high priests and the leaders said, "What more do we need to hear? We have all heard what He just said!"

They took Jesus away. They brought Him to the Roman governor of the city. His name was Pilate.

"This man says He is Christ a king," they told Pilate.

"Are you the King of the Jews?" Pilate asked Jesus.

"You have said sò," Jesus answered.

Pilate listened and wondered.

"I do not see what this man has done wrong," he said.

"He makes trouble," the priests and leaders said. "He stirs up the people from Galilee to Jerusalem."

"Does He come from Galilee?" asked Pilate.

And when he found Jesus did come from Galilee, Pilate was pleased. King Herod ruled Galilee, and the king was in Jerusalem at this time. He could decide what to do about Jesus.

Pilate sent Jesus to King Herod.

King Herod, too, asked Jesus many questions. But when Jesus would not answer him, the king was angry. He sent Jesus back to Pilate.

Then Pilate called the priests and leaders and people before him. "I have asked this man many questions," he said. "I still do not know what He has done wrong. I will let Him go free."

But the priests had made the people believe Jesus had done wrong. They did not want Jesus to go free. When Pilate saw that the people were growing angry, he said that Jesus must die.

Jesus and two other men were taken to a place called Calvary. Many people followed them. Some were very sad because they loved Jesus. Some women cried and cried.

At Calvary, Jesus was put on a cross. The two other men were put on crosses, too, one at either side of Jesus.

Jesus was very sad. He was sad for the people.

Jesus said, "Father, forgive them, for they know not what they do."

The long hours passed. At about the sixth hour of the day, a great darkness came over the land. The darkness lasted about three hours.

Then Jesus cried aloud. "Father," He cried, "into your hands I give my spirit."

162

In the evening, the friends of Jesus came. They took His body down from the cross. Their hearts were sad as they wrapped it in fine linen and laid it in a grave that was cut out from a rock. They rolled a great stone across the opening of the grave.

The women who had followed Jesus watched and wept.

Then a soldier was stationed there to guard the grave of Jesus so no one could take away His body.

LUKE 24:4-5 *Behold, two men stood by them in shining garments. And as they were afraid, and bowed down their faces to the earth, they said unto them, Why seek ye the living among the dead?*

Jesus Is Risen!

IT WAS the first day of the week after the crucifixion. Very early in the morning, some women who had loved Jesus and believed in Him went to the grave in the rock. They took perfume and oils to rub on His body. As they went, they cried softly for their friend and Master.

"How will we roll away the great, heavy stone before His grave?" they asked each other sadly.

But when they came to the grave, the great stone was already rolled away. And when the women went into the opening in the rock, His body was gone!

What had happened? Where was His body? The women could hardly believe what they saw.

Then suddenly, two men in shining robes appeared before them.

How frightened the women were!

But the shining ones said to them, "Why do you look for Jesus here? He is not here. He is alive again. Do you remember how He told you He would rise again?"

165

Then the women remembered. When Jesus was in Galilee, He had told them that He would rise again. Quickly, they went to the friends of Jesus, His disciples. They told them all they had seen.

Most of the disciples did not believe them. But John and Peter ran to the grave and saw that it was empty. They saw the linen that had been wrapped about the body of Jesus, but the body was gone. Wondering, they went away.

That same day, two of the disciples went to the village of Emmaus, a little way from Jerusalem. As they walked along, they talked of all that had happened. While they were talking, Jesus came near.

But the disciples did not know He was Jesus.

"What are you talking about?" Jesus asked them.

They looked at Him sadly.

"Don't you know what has happened to Jesus?" they asked. Then they told Him all that had happened.

When they drew near the village, Jesus started to leave them. But they asked Him to stay with them.

"It is growing late," they said. "Come eat with us."

Jesus went with them. As they sat at a table, He took the bread and blessed it. Then He broke it and gave it to them.

Then the disciples knew He was Jesus. But when they looked again, Jesus was gone.

At once, the two disciples started back to Jerusalem. They went to the other disciples.

"The Lord is risen," they told them.

While they were telling their friends how they had met Jesus on the road, Jesus Himself appeared before them.

"Peace be with you," He said.

The disciples were frightened. Was He a ghost?

But Jesus said, "Why are you frightened? Touch me and see I am alive. It is I myself."

The disciples were filled with joy. Jesus was with them
again! They were so happy they could hardly believe it
was true. While they wondered, Jesus spoke to them again.

"Have you anything to eat?" Jesus asked.

They gave Him broiled fish and some honey and Jesus ate
what they gave Him. Then they knew that Jesus was alive.

Jesus told them of God's wonderful plans. He helped
them understand why He had had to suffer to help make
these plans come true.

Then Jesus told His disciples to go all over the world
and tell people about God and Jesus.

"Teach them the things I tried to teach them," Jesus
said. "Remember that even though you do not see me, I
am with you always."

Then Jesus led His disciples to Bethany, and there He lifted up His hands and blessed them.

And while He blessed them, He parted from them and was carried up to heaven.

Then the disciples went back to Jerusalem with great joy and to the temple to praise God and give Him thanks.

Acts 2:1 *And when the day of Pentecost was fully come, they were all with one accord in one place.*

The Day of Pentecost

THERE WAS joy and happiness in the city of Jerusalem. The narrow streets were crowded with people from all parts of the kingdom.

For this was the day of Pentecost, the fiftieth day after the Passover. Pentecost was a very special day for the people of Israel. It was a harvest feast day, a day of thanksgiving.

"I will praise thee, O Lord!"

Long ago David, the shepherd king, had sung these words over and over again in his psalms, his songs of thanks to God. On this Pentecost day, many people in the streets of Jerusalem were also praising God for His goodness.

They had gathered together from many far away lands to celebrate the harvest feast. The homes and inns of the city were filled with guests and visitors.

"God is great! God is good!" they said, each in the language of his own country.

Feasts were being prepared, and there was happiness in the city.

169

But not all the people in the city were thinking with happiness of the harvest feast. The friends of Jesus, His disciples, were in Jerusalem, too. As they sat together in a room, they thought of Jesus. They thought of the sad things that had happened.

They talked of Jesus and of all He had taught them. They prayed together for strength and wisdom to teach the people about Jesus. And they remembered that Jesus had promised that He would be with them in all that they did.

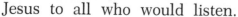

As they prayed, a wonderful thing happened. Suddenly a sound came from heaven like a mighty, rushing wind, and the room was filled with peace. A new radiance came to the disciples. They knew that the Holy Spirit was with them and they would not be alone in the work that they must do.

Peter stood up. His face shining, he gave thanks to God. Now the disciples were ready to tell the story of Jesus to all who would listen.

And when the disciples came out of the room, they found a great crowd gathered to watch them. Many in the crowd were from far away lands. But they had heard of these friends of Jesus.

Some in the crowd came to laugh at the disciples. But many others in the crowd waited quietly. When they saw the disciples, they were filled with wonder. For there was a shining light on the faces of all the disciples as if they had something wonderful to tell.

The crowd stirred. A murmur of voices filled the air.

Peter raised his hands, and the crowd grew still.

Then Peter told the story of Jesus.

He told it so simply and clearly that everyone in the crowd could understand.

There was no laughter now. Everyone listened to his words.

"The promise is to you and to your children," Peter said. "It is to people who are here and to people who are far away. It is to many, many people for it is to all who hear the message of God."

Many who listened heard God's message. Many who heard Peter's words came forward and were baptized.

Now Peter knew what he and the other disciples must do. They were to tell the story of Jesus to all the world.

ACTS 10:15   *And the voice spake unto him again the second time, What God hath cleansed, that call not thou common.*

Peter Has a Vision

PETER was one of the first disciples of Jesus. Always he loved Jesus and believed in Him. But sometimes while Jesus lived with the disciples, Peter had been weak or afraid.

Now Peter was sorry. He wanted to be strong and brave so he could go everywhere and tell people about Jesus. He wanted this so much that he grew brave and strong. He taught many people about Jesus.

One day Peter went up to the roof of a house where he was staying. It was noon and as Peter began to pray, he became very hungry. His friends went down to prepare food for him to eat.

But while Peter was alone on the roof of the house, he had a vision or a dream.

Peter saw the heavens open and something come down. It looked like a huge sheet. In the sheet were many kinds of animals. Some were wild animals. Some of the animals had four feet. Others were snakes that crawled. Still others were birds.

Then Peter heard a voice saying, "Rise, Peter. Kill the animals and eat them."

Peter was filled with wonder. These animals were the kinds Moses had told his people they must not eat because they were common or unclean. How could Peter eat them?

"No, Lord," Peter said. "I have never eaten anything that is common or unclean."

Then the voice spoke again.

"What God has cleaned," the voice said, "you must not call common."

This happened three times. Then the sheet with the animals in it rose again to heaven.

What did the vision mean? Peter wondered and wondered about it. While he wondered, three men came to the house.

"Is Peter here?" they asked.

Peter went down from the rooftop.

"I am Peter," he said. "What do you want of me?"

"A Roman soldier sent us," the three men told him. "An angel told him to ask you to come to his house and tell him about Jesus."

Peter was surprised. These men were not Jews. Until now, Peter had told only Jews about Jesus.

Then Peter remembered his vision. Was this why the vision had been sent to him? Did God want him to tell all kinds of people about Jesus?

Peter went to the home of the Roman soldier. Many people were gathered there. They were waiting for Peter.

These people were not Jews. But Peter told them about Jesus. As they listened, they believed in Jesus, too.

Peter knew now that God wanted people of every country to know about Him and Jesus.

After this, Peter and other disciples began to teach the people of all nations about Jesus. The wonderful news about Jesus was for all people everywhere.

174

ACTS 9:4 *And he fell to the earth, and heard a voice saying unto him, Saul, Saul, why persecutest thou me?*

For People Everywhere

PETER and the other disciples knew and loved Jesus. As Jesus had told them to do, they went and told the people about Jesus. They tried to teach what Jesus had taught them.

Then another man began to teach the people about Jesus. This man had never seen Jesus while He lived on earth. At first he did not believe in Jesus. He even fought against Him. But he became one of the best teachers about Jesus who ever lived.

How did this man change? How did he come to believe in Jesus? It happened in a strange and wonderful way.

The news about Jesus was being told in many parts of the country. More and more people listened. More and more people began to believe in Jesus. This made the high priests and the Romans angry.

They began to arrest the people who taught about Jesus and put them in prison.

One of the men who helped do this was called Saul or Paul. Paul was his Roman name.

Saul was a young man. He came from the city called Tarsus. He was proud of his city. He was proud of being a Jew and a Roman citizen. Saul did not believe in Jesus. He thought it was wrong to teach the people to believe in Jesus.

Saul traveled from place to place. He tried to find the men who were teaching the people about Jesus. He wanted to put them all in prison, for he thought they were doing wrong.

One day Saul started off to visit the city of Damascus. He planned to go to the Jewish temples there. If he found any of the disciples of Jesus, he would take them back to Jerusalem and have them put in prison.

As Saul and his men came near Damascus, a bright light was suddenly all around him. The light was so bright it hurt Saul's eyes. He fell to the ground and hid his face from the dazzling brightness.

As he fell, he heard a voice saying, "Saul, Saul, why do you fight against me?"

"Who are you, Lord?" asked Saul, trembling.

The voice answered, "I am Jesus."

Saul trembled even more. "What do you want me to do?" he asked.

Jesus said, "Go into the city. You will be told what to do."

The men with Saul were frightened, too. They could hear a voice. But they could not see who was speaking.

Saul stumbled to his feet. He opened his eyes, but he could not see. The light had blinded him.

Saul's men took him by the hands and led him into the city of Damascus. They led him to a house where he could stay.

For three days, Saul stayed in this house. He could not see, for he was still blinded. He did not eat or drink.

Saul waited for Jesus to let him know what to do.

Then Jesus sent one of His disciples to Saul. This man was called Ananias, and he lived in Damascus.

"Saul," Ananias said to him. "Jesus has sent me to you. Now you will see again."

And suddenly Saul could see again! He could see the sunlight and the blue sky. He could see the world around him. How fresh and new and beautiful everything looked! Can you imagine how happy and thankful Saul was?

Now Saul knew he had been wrong to fight Jesus. Now he believed in Jesus. He wanted all the people to believe, too. He knew now what Jesus wanted him to do.

Saul began to tell the people of Damascus about Jesus.

How surprised the people were as they listened to him! They knew how Saul had put men in prison for teaching about Jesus. But as they listened to him, they saw how he was changed. They saw that he really believed in Jesus now.

The rulers of the city were angry when they heard what Saul was doing. They planned to catch him when he went out of the city. They had the gates of the city watched day and night.

Saul heard about this. How could he get out of the city safely? He and his friends made a brave plan.

When he was ready to leave the city, he did not go out of the gates. He waited until it was night.

Then, in the darkness, Saul got into a big basket. And slowly and carefully, his friends let the basket down, over the city wall!

Saul was outside the city. He was safe!

As time went on, Saul traveled to many places. He was put in prison sometimes, but always he went on telling the people about Jesus, for he knew the wonderful news was for people everywhere.

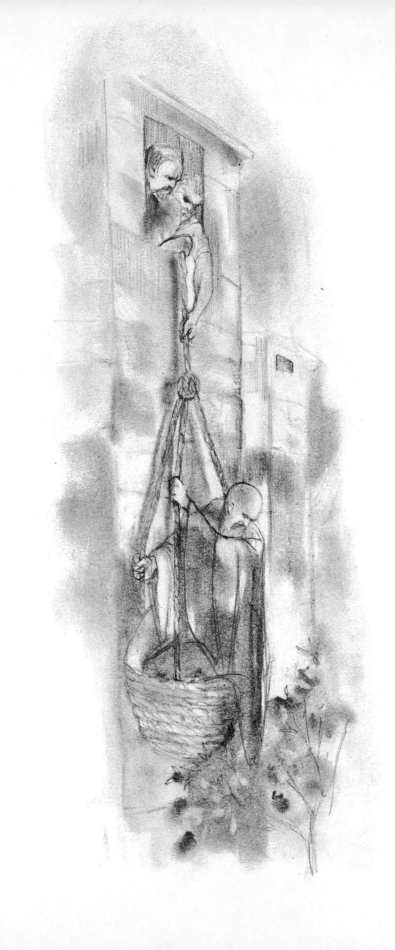

Prayers and Graces

He prayeth best who loveth best
All things both great and small;
For the dear God who loveth us,
He made and loveth all.

SAMUEL TAYLOR COLERIDGE

180

This is the day
Which the Lord hath made;
We will rejoice
And be glad in it.

THE BIBLE: PSALM 118:24

I will praise Thee, O Lord,
With my whole heart;
I will show forth
All Thy marvelous works.

I will be glad
And rejoice in Thee:
I will sing praise
To Thy name,
O Thou Most High.

THE BIBLE: PSALM 9:1-2

Father of all, in heaven above,
        We thank Thee for Thy love . . .

Father, we thank Thee for the night,
And for the pleasant morning light,
For rest and food and loving care,
And all that makes the world so fair.

Help us to do the things we should,
To be to others kind and good,
In all we do, in all we say,
To grow more loving day by day.

We thank Thee for the world so sweet,
We thank Thee for the food we eat,
We thank Thee for the birds that sing,
We thank Thee, Lord, for everything.

God is so good that He will hear,
  Whenever little children pray;
He always lends a gracious ear
  To what the youngest child may say.

His own most holy Book declares
  He loveth little children still;
And that He listens to their prayers
  Just as a tender father will.

JANE TAYLOR

All things bright and beautiful,
All creatures great and small,
All things wise and wonderful,
The Lord God made them all.

Each little flower that opens,
Each little bird that sings,
He made their glowing colors,
He made their tiny wings.

CECIL FRANCES ALEXANDER

I hear no voice, I feel no touch,
  I see no glory bright;
But yet I know that God is near,
  In darkness as in light.

He watches ever by my side,
  And hears my whispered prayer;
The Father for His little child
  Each night and day doth care.

Bless us, Lord, we humbly pray,
            Guide and help us through the day . . .

Heavenly Father, hear our prayer,
Keep us in Thy loving care.
Guard us through the livelong day,
In our work and in our play.
Keep us pure and sweet and true
In everything we say and do.

Dear Father, hear and bless
Thy beasts and singing birds
And guard with tenderness
Small things that have no words.

May the strength of God pilot us,
May the power of God preserve us,
May the wisdom of God instruct us,
May the hand of God protect us.

God be in my head,
   And in my understanding;
God be in mine eyes,
   And in my looking;
God be in my mouth,
   And in my speaking;
God be in my heart,
   And in my thinking.

SARUM PRIMER, 1558

When I run about all day,
When I kneel at night to pray,
   God sees.

When I'm dreaming in the dark,
When I lie awake and hark,
   God sees.

Need I ever know a fear?
Night and day my Father's near—
   God sees.

MARY MAPES DODGE

For what we are about to receive,
        The Lord make us truly grateful . . .

Bless, O Lord, this food to our use,
And us to Thy loving service.

Thou art great, Lord,
Thou art good,
And we thank Thee
For our food.
By Thy hand
Must all be fed,
We thank Thee
For our daily bread.

God is Love,
God is Good,
And we thank Him
For our food.

Some hae meat and canna eat,
  And some wad eat that want it;
But we hae meat and we can eat,
  And sae the Lord be thankit.

ROBERT BURNS

Here a little child I stand,
Heaving up my either hand,
Cold as paddocks though they be,
Here I lift them up to Thee,
For a benison to fall
On our meat and on us all.

ROBERT HERRICK

Bless these Thy gifts,
Most gracious God,
From whom all goodness springs;
Make clean our hearts
And feed our souls
With good and joyful things.

187

The Lord bless us and keep us
This night and always . . .

Now I lay me down to sleep,
I pray Thee, Lord, my soul to keep;
And when I wake, dear Lord, I pray,
Bless and guide me through the day.

Loving Jesus, meek and mild,
Look upon a little child!

Make me gentle as Thou art,
Come and live within my heart.

Take my childish hand in Thine,
Guide these little feet of mine.

Jesus, tender Shepherd, hear me,
Bless Thy little lamb tonight;
Through the darkness be Thou near me,
Keep me safe till morning light.

188

Watch Thou, dear Lord,
With those who wake,
Or watch, or weep tonight,
And give Thine angels charge
Over those who sleep.

Matthew, Mark,
Luke, and John,
Bless the bed
I lie upon.
Four corners
To my bed,
Four angels
Round my head:
One to sing,
And one to pray,
And two to watch
Until the day.

Lord, we thank Thee for the night,
Keep us safe till morning light,
As the shepherd in his fold
Keeps his sheep from harm and cold.

Bless the friends we hold so dear,
Father, Mother, and all here.
And may Thy little children be
Ever very near to Thee.

Good night! Good night!
Far flies the light;
But still God's love
Shall flame above,
Making all bright.
Good night!
        Good night!

VICTOR HUGO

Now the day is over,
  Night is drawing nigh,
Shadows of the evening
  Steal across the sky.

When the morning wakens,
  Then may I arise,
Fresh and pure and sinless
  In Thy holy eyes.

The Lord is my shepherd;
I shall not want.
He maketh me to lie down in green pastures:
He leadeth me beside the still waters.
He restoreth my soul:
He leadeth me in the paths of righteousness
For His name's sake.
Yea, though I walk through the valley
Of the shadow of death,
I will fear no evil:
For Thou art with me;
Thy rod and Thy staff
They comfort me.
Thou preparest a table before me
In the presence of mine enemies:
Thou anointest my head with oil;
My cup runneth over.
Surely goodness and mercy shall follow me
All the days of my life:
And I will dwell in the house of the Lord
For ever.

THE BIBLE: PSALM 23

DESIGN: WILLIS PROUDFOOT

LETTERING: PHIL DOERN

LITHOGRAPHY: AMERICAN LITHO ARTS, INC.

PRINTING: VON HOFFMAN PRESS, INC.